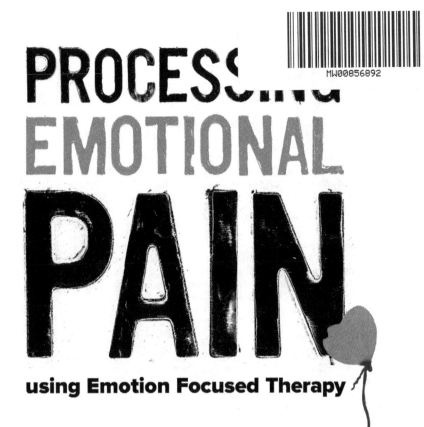

PROCESSING EMOTIONAL PAIN

using Emotion Focused Therapy

A guide to safely working
with and resolving emotional
injuries and trauma

Dr Melissa Harte

AUSTRALIANACADEMIC**PRESS**

First published 2019 by:
Australian Academic Press Group Pty. Ltd.
Samford Valley QLD, Australia
www.australianacademicpress.com.au

 A catalogue record for this book is available from the National Library of Australia

Processing emotional pain using emotion focused therapy:
A guide to safely working with and resolving emotional injuries and trauma
ISBN 9781925644333 (paperback)
ISBN 9781925644340 (ebook)

Disclaimer
Every effort has been made in preparing this work to provide information based on accepted standards and practice at the time of publication. The publisher and author, however, make no representations or warranties with respect to the accuracy or completeness of the contents of this book and specifically disclaim any implied warranties of merchantability or fitness for a particular purpose. It is sold on the understanding that the publisher is not engaged in rendering professional services and neither the publisher nor the author shall be liable for damages arising herefrom. If professional advice or other expert assistance is required, the services of a competent professional should be sought.

Publisher & Editor: Stephen May

Cover design: Luke Harris, Working Type Studio

Typesetting: Australian Academic Press

Printing: Lightning Source

Contents

Chapter 4 — The highly sensitive person phenomena

Chapter 5 — Emotion Focused Therapy: An overview

As with most books, they are not solely created by the author. There is often a silent but vital group of people who contribute in all sorts of ways. This is my tribute to those people who have believed in me and encouraged me even when I had lost faith in myself.

Many people have said 'you should write a book' but I would agree, laugh and then completely dismiss the idea. But these voices persisted in a way that was actually encouraging. I was my own worst critic. 'Do I have anything worthwhile to write about?'.

A wonderful woman, Erica Frydenberg, thought I did. She saw me present at the Australian Psychological Society (APS) Congress in 2016 and felt what I was saying had to be documented in a book. She has written a number of books herself and was very gracious and showed me the mechanics of how to put a book together. She also introduced me to Stephen May, publisher at Australian Academic Press. I sent him a rough draft and he accepted the proposal in mid-2017.

Over the ten years of working as a therapist using Emotion Focused Therapy (EFT) I had started putting ideas together and wrote them down in random documents. My filing system for such things is very haphazard.

When I had a health scare in January 2018 my crew of enthusiasts become louder and more insistent that I begin writing. They were concerned that if I died all my knowledge would die with me. So, I took heed and began to take their suggestions more seriously.

The concepts of the book were in my head. I just needed to find a way to get them out. I had done some research in my doctoral thesis and more in my master's so that seemed a good place to start. I had tried in vain to get any of my research published and so felt discouraged that my book had no real authenticity.

During the beginning of 2018, I was so busy trying to stay alive and pay my bills that I also couldn't imagine finding the space and time to be creative.

I needed a change of scenery.

I have been spending my summer holidays in a place called Cape Paterson, near Wonthaggi in Gippsland, Victoria. On a whim, I decided to attend a working bee one cold August Saturday morning. I needed to do something completely different. I met some amazing people as we planted 500 trees in the rain.

I clicked with two ladies in particular: Leone and Lesley. I also met Leone's long-term partner, Mike, and Lesley's husband Barry. I felt I had found my tribe. It's hard as a psychologist to meet new friends. Most of the people you deeply connect with are fellow psychologists. Other people think you are trying to psychoanalyse them. So, this meeting was particularly significant for me.

Leone asked if I was driving the two hours back to Melbourne that day and I said I actually had rented a place for the night. She said I should have stayed with them. I had only just met her. She told me that she and Mike were off on holidays for the next month and would I like to house sit. Such unconditional generosity.

So, I agreed and decided this was my retreat opportunity to write my book.

I gathered my laptop, some books and papers and set off for a five-day weekend in mid-September, 2018. It was freezing cold and I kept warm with a wood-fired heater going all day and all night. Sorry, Mike, I used all your wood. The house has a lovely sunny spot to sit and I settled in to write. Thanks, dear Leone and Mike. You have become true friends.

When I looked at my skeleton of a book and went searching for the material I had written, I found I actually had seven of the nine chapters already in draft. I was so surprised that it was all there. I began to write the preface, which was challenging, added to existing writings and wrote the missing ones.

I happened to be at an APS dinner in late 2018 and was telling Bruce Stevens of my book. He was very encouraging and suggested a good editor. He said that would be expensive. Bother I thought. Because of my health issues and reduced income, I quickly found I couldn't afford him.

What to do? Fortunately, I am an expert problem-solver. Being a single mum for 17 years raising three children and re-educating myself helped me to become very resourceful. So asked my team of enthusiasts (the voices) to edit a chapter each. They did it graciously and enthusiastically.

So, thank you Ash, Barry, Lou, Gen, Vivienne, Anthony and Matthew. I appreciate you all so much. Your voices helped me get it done. Without your encouragement and support this book would not exist. I would also like to thank all the EFT trainees who wanted more of what I said. As a final edit, Matthew suggested a lovely woman Jenny Valentish who did a final content edit. She was and is excellent.

There are two friends, who have become part of my chosen family, that I need to thank as well: Heike and Mary have watched my career unfold and have been there when things got tough. I know we have had our ups and downs, as true families do, but I do appreciate you both very much. Thank you.

Last, but not least, I want to thank my children who supported my determination to re-educate myself and have loved me despite my absences at university and conferences. My commitment to your growth and development has been a huge motivation for me. I wanted you to have a family life that included love and acceptance. You have given me that in return.

Thank you to you all. It's been a huge journey.

Dr Melissa Harte MAPS FCCOUNP

x

I imagine people who write such a book as this have their own story to tell. I am no different. There have been many personal and professional experiences that have influenced my journey into psychology and counselling. As I reflected on the process of writing this book, I realised that *emotional pain* was something that I became curious about a very long time ago. I certainly didn't use that language but I knew what it was like to feel emotional pain. As a child I did not understand concepts such as trauma, attachment injury, depression, anxiety and post-traumatic stress. But I did know that I was adopted at ten days old. And I knew about sore throats that led to illnesses like tonsillitis and operations like tonsillectomies, as I had one when I was six years old. I knew how horrible it was to be alone in a large hospital in 1965 when parents just left you there. I also didn't know that the behaviour perpetrated by my adopted father was sexual abuse. I knew about death because my adopted father died when I was eleven, having succumbed to bladder cancer. He had been unwell for two years. My mother was devastated and debilitated. I did not understand grief and loss. I knew about breast cancer because both my adopted mother and her mother had mastectomies. I knew that I had to draw on resources of learning how to cope on my own and look after myself as my mother was unable. I didn't know about emotional neglect.

As a teenager I was left to my own devices and was given a great amount of freedom. I was clever at school and considered very responsible. At sixteen, I didn't know that when you said 'no' to sex but it happened anyway it was date rape. Inside, I felt insecure and lost, and was experiencing what I now have come to know was emotional pain. I craved to be part of a group but I did not understand that my family was different from other families. I certainly felt marginalised because I had no father, but I also had a mother who had a hidden mental health issue. Not long before her death a few years ago it was discovered she had schizophrenia. This information was kept from my sister, the natural child of my adopted parents, and from me. From an early age I knew I wanted to be a doctor. I wanted to understand how to make people feel better.

For the next 25 years I found myself in very unsuitable and abusive relationships. My attempt to get into medicine was thwarted when I fell in love in my Year 12 and lost myself in the relationship. I was by sheer chance able to get into a medical laboratory science course at RMIT. I did not really enjoy the course and only just passed. That Year 12 relationship didn't last. Severe depression and what I now know to be chronic fatigue set in. I could not understand why I felt so terrible all the time. I slept eighteen hours a day. I told my mother I was not coping. Her brother was a GP and he suggested that I consult a psychiatrist. This man wanted to put me on antidepressants and was quite dismissive of me when I refused. He invited me back the next week for a follow-up session but could not remember any of the things that I had told him the week before. I never went back. Over the years I have engaged in various forms of counselling with varying degrees of success; alternative health practices, kinesiology and read every self-help book I could lay my hands on, to help me understand this emotional pain that I had felt most of my life. I even engaged in primal therapy after reading *The Primal Scream* by Arthur Janov (1973).

My working life began at 15 when I was employed at the Myer store as a retail assistant in the cosmetic department. I worked there for 4 years. At 19 years old, and during my studies at RMIT, I worked in hospitality. After finishing my degree I worked as a histologist as a medical laboratory scientist in various hospitals and private laboratories. I was good at it and enjoyed the work of producing paraffin slides and staining them to show the cellular degeneration. However, I was very disillusioned by the medical profession and found working in the field of pathology very disconcerting. I wanted to be a doctor to prevent disease, not identify it when it had already occurred. I left the medical laboratory field to have my first child. In the years that followed I worked in all sorts of odd jobs that ranged from selling showers screens, doing office administration, retail, and even was restaurant owner for three years.

After the birth of my third child when I was 40 years old, I realised I needed to do something with my life. I left my (now what I know was) narcissistic third husband and moved with my children to a very small rental on the outer suburbs of Melbourne. I survived on a single mother's pension from Centrelink and decided to return to study. Fortunately, the old science degree that I had done at RMIT was recognised by Monash University and I was credited to be able to complete a graduate diploma in psychology over the next three years, obtaining extremely good marks. I had finally found the career that was to give meaning to my life. After the graduate diploma I headed off to The University of Melbourne where I did honours over two years. I then went to La Trobe University to do a doctorate in Counselling Psychology. It was there that I started to begin to understand how a person's past history can impact his or her current experience.

I have heard it said that some people enter the field of psychology to understand themselves. I agree with this. Pieces of the puzzle started to come together and I began to make sense of my experiences and see my life from a broader perspective. The multilayered traumas that I had experienced had impacted on my ability to create secure relationships and had hindered my psychological development. In addition, I had struggled to find good therapists or psychologists that understood me in the context of my family and childhood history. I hadn't realised that my childhood history had any bearing on my mental and emotional state. As I embarked on my doctoral research, I began to understand this more fully.

At La Trobe University I was first introduced to the person centred approach, developed by Carl Rogers. I now call him my greatest teacher. The necessary and sufficient conditions to create a good working alliance in therapy (empathy, congruence and unconditional positive regard) showed me how to connect to others. This was a revelation to me. I was surprised that a private Catholic school education and a more than average intelligence had not taught me how to create respectful, authentic and connected relationships. At La Trobe I was also introduced to Emotion Focused Therapy (EFT). This modality gave me another framework to help me understand how early attachment injuries and trauma impact the developing human being and their emotional intelligence.

My doctoral thesis was a qualitative investigation into the necessary and sufficient components that led to change for four young women (aged 18 to

25) with depression. Comorbid anxiety was present in each of the four women, who had a history of unresolved events and/or trauma that had resulted in enduring emotional pain.

Each young woman was offered a minimum of twelve EFT counselling sessions with me. All sessions were recorded and transcribed. The intense nature of the investigation assisted me to begin to understand those 'moments of change' and what components were necessary to precipitate that change. In recent times I undertook a Master's in Clinical Psychology at Swinburne University of Technology. The model that I present to you in this book originated from my doctoral research that was later refined using task analysis as part of my master's research.

So, at 60 years old, I find I have become a doctor and a teacher but not quite in the way I had envisaged. I am a doctor of psychology, not a doctor of medicine, and an internationally accredited EFT trainer. I dedicate this book to all those practitioners and clients who have experienced emotional pain in their lives, who need to be understood in the context of those experiences and to provide a framework and a model that works gently, effectively and deeply to assist in reversing the resultant psychological, emotional, spiritual and physical damage.

This book is written for practitioners who work with clients that have experienced emotional pain. This pain may be attachment related, be a single episode or the culmination of many so called 'small t trauma' events that have left their clients with emotional pain that still impacts their lives despite valiant attempts to resolve them or deny them.

It is possible to choose chapters at random but the book is best read sequentially as each chapter builds on information from the previous chapter in the same way the model was developed. This is a 'how to' book, presenting techniques and concepts to assist practitioners. Of course, a book such as this cannot replace the benefits of experiential learning but it is nevertheless a useful reference and guide. Please note that the people mentioned in the case studies in this book gave consent to be included and have all been de-identified.

In Chapter 1, I raise the important issue of how, until very recently, impacts of trauma were often overlooked or minimised when formalising case histories. This could lead to important background information being missed, inappropriate psychological assessments, erroneous interpretations and diagnoses and possibly inappropriate treatment. This is illustrated in a client case study called 'Gary'. Fortunately, we are seeing new trends and more accurate understanding of how to identify trauma and its impact.

Chapter 2 highlights the dilemma with the DSM-5 diagnostic criteria for Post-Traumatic Stress Disorder (PTSD). Two cases, Maria and Mike, are discussed in terms of different aetiologies and presentations. In Chapter 3, I address the value of understanding the importance of emotions and how, as adaptive experiences, they provide important information that can assist us in our daily lives.

The majority of clients that consult with me show traits of high sensitivity. In Chapter 4, I discuss the trait of high sensitivity and ask the question: 'Are you or your clients highly sensitive?'. This concept helps to depathologise many of the assumptions made about sensitivity.

EFT is a very comprehensive model. It has been developed through vigorous research and is listed as an evidence-based treatment for depression on the American Psychological Association website. There has been much written, and randomised control trials conducted, that identifies EFT's effectiveness for treatment of trauma (Paivio & Pascual-Leone, 2010), generalised anxiety (Watson & Greenberg, 2017; Watson, Timulak, & Greenberg, 2019), borderline personality disorder (Warwar, Links, Greenberg, & Bergmans, 2008) and social anxiety (Elliott & Shahar, 2017; Shahar, Bar-Kalifa, & Alon, 2017) and there is good evidence for its effectiveness in treating eating disorders (Dolhanty & Greenberg, 2007, 2009; Dolhanty & Lafrance, 2019). Having worked predominantly with this model for over ten years and as an internationally accredited EFT trainer who has trained over 500 practitioners in the model, there is no doubt in my mind that EFT is a very effective treatment. There is also no doubt that the complexity of this model means it is not for everyone. It requires the therapist to have done some of their own therapeutic work and be willing to sit with and navigate through the often intense emotional experiences of their clients.

Chapter 5 endeavours to provide a simplified overview of EFT. In Chapter 6, I explain the concepts of emotional pain and how to work through it with an extended version of the EFT task of focusing. I share with the reader how this task was developed, highlight the influences that helped to shape the task and discuss the various significant components. I describe the task analysis research I undertook that was used to develop the extended focusing task. In Chapter 7, I introduce the reader to the challenges around identifying dissociation and how to manage it in session. The grounding and safe place technique is introduced and discussed in detail as an integral part of assisting clients to stay present to their experience so they can integrate the new information that may occur in session. This chapter also presents a case from my own research, 'John and Betty', which illustrates the steps of the task.

When I think about working with clients who have experienced painful or traumatic events resulting in emotional pain, my first instinct is to work with them to build their sense of self. In my experience this is most effectively managed with the extended focusing task. However, there comes a time later in therapy where the inter-psychic elements need to be addressed. In Chapter 8, I discuss using chair work as another element of working through emotional pain. Later in therapy the client is more robust and therefore likely to be more willing to engage in the chair work. I conclude the book with a proposed meta-perspective, about how people get stuck in certain patterns of behaviour and how therapy and other forms of personal development can effect change so that they can come to live a 'more aware' life. Emotional pain is part of most people's realities, and identifying it and working through it can lead to living fulfilling and emotionally rich lives.

I hope you enjoy reading this book and can take from the contents of these pages safe and useful ways of working with people who have emotional pain.

Introduction

O ver the past ten years, it has become increasingly evident that experiencing trauma is more common than many of us realised. Finally, in large part thanks to the writings and teachings of trauma therapists such as Bessel van der Kolk (1993, 1994, 1995, 2005; van der Kolk & Fisler, 1994), Babette Rothschild (2011), John Briere (2014), Pat Ogden (2006; Ogden & Fisher, 2015), Sandra Paivio (2010) and Judith Herman (1993), there is more understanding and appreciation for the nature of trauma.

The word trauma can be used to describe both a cause and an impact. In other words, trauma can be defined both as the act of, and experience of, a distressing event. There are many types of trauma experiences, ranging from what may appear fairly benign but still significant to the person (such as an emotional injury occurring within an interpersonal relationship), to a more obviously severe, single-incident trauma (such as rape), to the most complex, developmental trauma that results in significant ramifications to the emerging personality (such as persistent physical abuse of a child by a parent). An *emotional injury* occurs in situations where the biologically adaptive response of primary emotion is inhibited or restricted; and, when this happens, the fulfilment of basic human needs to be loved, validated and safe, are prevented or violated. An injury of this kind has an enduring quality experienced as *emotional pain* that burdens a person long after the event, as though a wound has not healed. Emotional pain is the unpleasant, overwhelming, upsetting internal experience or "response to an injury that prevents or violates the fulfilment of the basic human needs of being loved, safe and acknowledged" (Timulak, 2015, p. 2). The emotional pain can be experienced as a physical pain as well as psychological.

A few years ago, a 26-year-old motor mechanic (let's call him Gary) consulted me. He presented with anxiety and depression and had been apprehended by the police while trying to dispose of a car to get the insurance money. He was given a suspended sentence due to the fact that he had no prior offences. Things escalated as he had breached a court order for community service.

Gary regularly attended sessions with a clinical psychologist for about two years prior to seeing me. The psychologist was asked to assess Gary's psychological state during and after the offence and provide a written report for the court. The psychologist described Gary as nonconforming, belligerent, and having issues with authority figures. Fortunately, his mother was very proactive and refused to accept the findings of the psychologist. She knew that despite being on medication, he was very depressed and she was concerned about his well-being. She went searching for a psychologist in the area where her son lived and came across me.

When I first met Gary, his new court case was looming. Thankfully, I had not read the report from the previous psychologist and was free to make my own assessment. Upon collecting information about Gary's family and personal history, I identified that he had come from a relatively stable home and that his family was caring and strongly supportive of him. He was an identical twin, and the boys had a very close relationship. He also had an older sister. In the recent past, he was having relationship difficulties with his partner of seven years, culminating in their separation. Their son was nearly four and another child was on the way.

After much encouragement, Gary explained to me that three years previously he had a trail bike accident. He had been riding in the remote bushland and fallen off. He lay on the ground, unable to move, for some time before his mates found him. He was taken by ambulance to the nearest hospital and was treated for a broken neck.

Before his accident, Gary was functioning at a more-than-competent level, which allowed him to feel confident enough to embark on the often risky venture of being self-employed and running his own motor mechanic business. He described getting to work early and being conscientious, making coffee for everyone, interacting with his fellow workers as "mates" and really "getting through the work". He was attentive to his partner and they enjoyed each other's company. They had bought a house and were looking forward to a good life together. He took the responsibility of caring and supporting his family very seriously. In addition, his general manner and activities prior to the accident could be described as pro-social. He had a close family network, a large number of friends, and a willingness to be of assistance to the general public by employing people in his own business.

After the accident, Gary's head was placed in a 'halo', and for twelve months he was unable to work or contribute to his own care or that of his family or his business. He remembered every aspect of the accident in graphic detail, and when he thought about it he experienced intense psychological pain. Despite having ridden motorbikes since he was four years old, Gary was not only reluctant to ride again but extremely fearful of doing so. He was able to rationally consider the idea of riding still but unable to actually ride because of the anxiety reaction evoked by considering it. He felt unable to go out in public while wearing the halo and wanted to just stay at home and hide from the world. He felt like a "paralysed, useless person", and described the experience of wearing the halo as "physically and mentally bringing you down". Further, any neck or lower back pain he experienced triggered memories of the accident, and that reminder was experienced within his body as "shocks" or "jolts".

During the twelve months following his accident, Gary's business underwent significant difficulties without his presence. He had not been able to sleep, had become hypervigilant, and his relationship had deteriorated. Doctors prescribed medication and suggested that he see a psychologist. He started consulting that clinical psychologist eleven months after the accident and a few months before the separation with his partner. The reason for consulting the psychologist was because of the stress he was experiencing in his relationship, and as a result of working long hours in his business to make up for the time he was away convalescing.

Gary had overcompensated for not having worked for twelve months by putting in extremely long hours at work to save his business. He thought he was doing the right thing by his family, but in his diminished state he was working hard but not necessarily "smart". Gary was obsessed with working extremely hard and for long hours in order to ensure the success of his business. The irony was that he knew the business was providing a reasonably stable income for his family and could sustain the employment of three others.

In addition, Gary was emotionally numb, had diminished interest and participation in significant activities, felt detached from important people in his life, experienced a restricted range of affect (mainly only anger and sadness) and very little enjoyment in life, and had a sense of foreboding about what he saw as the inevitable failure of his business. He described experiences in the previous two years where he felt like "life is going on around me, but I am not part of it ... like I am that lamp there, but not really *here*". He tried to avoid thinking or talking about the accident, yet customers would often ask him about it, giving him more of the "shock reminders" in his body.

Gary's inability to connect with the important people in his life, such as his partner, predisposed her to have an affair. The affair was in progress for three months before they broke up and he was "totally unaware anything was going on". The breakdown of his relationship compounded his already diminished state of mind, and he became very depressed and suicidal. His ability to focus on his work became challenging, he lost interest in everything, and he did not go out or speak to anyone. He struggled to solve problems and lacked the necessary motivation to achieve his goals. He lost his licence for speeding and started drinking as a way to deal with his physical and emotional pain. He had little regard for negative consequences when in this state of mind. Asked about his motivation for disposing of the car, he shrugged his shoulders; he was at a loss to explain what had possessed him to take such action. It is likely that in his diminished and decompensated state his accomplice's suggestion that they "ditch the car for the insurance money" seemed an easy way out of yet another complicated and overwhelming situation that he felt unable to solve more appropriately.

Gary grew increasing agitated after the accident. He required medication to sleep, had outbursts of anger and irritability that were increasingly more frequent, and his anxiety and stress levels made it difficult to concentrate and not overthink things. More specifically, he experienced an overwhelming sense of fear of loss, which was projected away from himself and onto the possible loss of his business and resulting financial insecurity. This was also seen in the fact he would "do anything" for his partner and son.

For most of us reading this case, it is clear that Gary was suffering from Post-Traumatic Stress Disorder (PTSD). The fact that the clinical psychologist missed these vital pieces of information concerned me. The psychologist had identified current symptoms without considering the context of Gary's recent and historical past. This was a young man working hard to create a business and provide for his young family. If Gary had received the appropriate treatment at the time, his partner might not have sought comfort elsewhere, he may not have nearly lost his business, and I suspect that his quality of life over the previous three years would certainly have been a great deal better.

When I asked Gary about his experience with the clinical psychologist, he reported that the form of counselling involved a great deal of advice-giving from the psychologist. He described often feeling "intimidated", and that all in all it was not very helpful. Despite attending fairly regularly, he did not find his depression was lifting. I suspect the treatment did not work because his depression and anxiety were the result of his PTSD. The prescribed medication was also not working because the aim of antidepressants is to treat depression and not PTSD.

The treatment that I provided Gary involved a process of working through that traumatic event, but in a particular way that did not require him to talk about the incident in great detail and thus not become retraumatised by the remembering of it. Interestingly enough, he did not have the language to explain his experience, and thus found he was unable to describe the incident sufficiently to *talk* it through. The core emotional pain was that Gary remembered lying there on the ground, unable to move and uncertain as to what his future would look like. More pressingly, he thought he might die. The therapeutic process that I will describe in further detail in Chapter 7 enabled him to experience the core emotional pain in such a way that he was not overwhelmed by it and he could integrate the reality that he survived, rather than remaining in the same hypervigilant, traumatised state that he had been in for the past three years.

This story gives a simple illustration of the importance of understanding trauma and its impact. We need to be trauma-informed and learn how to identify signs and symptoms as well as how to work with the subtle nuances that we so often see when trauma presents. In this case, it was a single incident of trauma, but because it was overlooked, it led to a series of complications. Those with 'complex' or 'developmental' trauma (van der Kolk, 1994, 1995, 2005), involving chronic interpersonal traumatic experiences in childhood, require very specialised and gentle processing of their experience. The model presented in this book will illustrate a unique, powerful, and evidence-based way to do this.

Two cases of Post-Traumatic Stress Disorder (PTSD)

There has been a great deal of confusion about how trauma is conceptualised and diagnosed. I would like to present two cases that both warrant the diagnosis of Post-Traumatic Stress Disorder (PTSD) and yet have very different aetiologies.

How can that be? Well, the current Diagnostic Statistical Manual, 5th edition (DSM 5) states it is not concerned with causation and instead offers a set of criteria to categorise mental health conditions to determine a diagnostic label:

> Since a complete description of the underlying pathological processes is not possible for most mental disorders, it is important to emphasise that the current diagnostic criteria are the best available description of how mental disorders are expressed and can be recognised by trained clinicians (American Psychiatric Association, 2013; p. xii).

Paradoxically, built into the criteria of PTSD is the fact that its cause is as a result of exposure to overwhelming stress — but it still falls short of being more specific. For instance, the cause of overwhelming stress can be as varied as witnessing an accident in a matter of minutes, or enduring prolonged abuse.

I wish to challenge the DSM typography of PTSD for complex trauma clients, as did Judith Herman (1992); (Herman, 2012; Lindauer, 2012; van der Kolk, 2005). I believe that *complex PTSD*, or the more appropriately named *developmental trauma disorder* (van der Kolk, 2005), is a distinct and separate disorder that should not be considered in the same way as the more conventional PTSD as described in DSM 5.

The two cases I present highlight that the omission of context when coming to understand a case presentation may actually interfere with treatment options, in that they miss important client considerations and may not be in the best interests of the client.

Mick and Maria (not their real names) have been chosen because they represent characteristic histories of clients who experience symptom patterns described as PSTD. The information about Maria was sourced from the internet and Mick's case has been sourced from a practitioner who works with veterans (permission was granted to use this information). The cases represent the types of 'typical' clients who present with PTSD.

Mick

Mick, a 44-year-old Army veteran, lives at home with his wife and three young children. Mick is currently on extended medical absence following his most recent deployment to Afghanistan.

Mick led a small unit of combat engineers who were responsible for detecting and clearing improvised explosive devices (IEDs). One day on a routine patrol, one of the team triggered an IED, amputating his lower leg and hand. Mick and two other officers administered first aid while they waited for air support to arrive, but he later learned that the man did not survive.

After being debriefed, Mick returned to duty, saying he was 'fine' and eager to get back to the job at hand. Although he barely slept in the weeks following the incident, he brushed it off as 'par for the course' whilst on deployment and 'just cracked on'. However, Mick grew increasingly impatient and heavy-handed with his junior officers. After making an out-of-character navigational error on patrol, he was assessed as medically unfit and sent back to Australia.

Mick was initially happy to be back with his family, but soon found that he couldn't be around them for very long before feeling the urge to withdraw to the shed. His sleep worsened and he started having nightmares in which he felt helpless. He described moments of 'feeling like I'm not here anymore, like I'm back there... like I'm going to puke, wondering when the fucking help is going to arrive'. Most nights, when his children were asleep, Mick would quietly enter their rooms and check that they had all their limbs intact. Says Mick: 'I felt like I was losing my fucking mind'.

Maria

Maria, a 26-year-old woman at the time of entering therapy, lived with her partner of four years and worked as an administrative assistant. She was the eldest of three children. Her mother separated from her father when she was an infant. During Maria's childhood, her mother had two subsequent de-facto relationships: Leslie and Ian.

Maria was sexually abused by both of these men over a period of approximately eight years. Between the ages of five and eight, she was abused by Leslie, who had alcohol dependence, and forced her to assist him masturbate. Maria reported that she can remember feeling very uncomfortable, stating: 'I felt that it was wrong, but shut myself off afterwards and pretended I was somewhere else ... At the time, like, I was in two minds because I was thinking that I felt uncomfortable doing it. It felt really wrong but perhaps it's okay because he seems okay with it.'

There were many arguments between her mother and Leslie, and Maria witnessed him punch her mother in the face. Maria reported that her mother was always absent from the home during the abuse.

Maria was later also sexually abused between the ages of eight and twelve by her mother's next partner, Ian. Maria reported that Ian 'made me touch his penis. It happened a fair bit over time, but I just remember a few bits and pieces.' Ian also touched Maria inappropriately around the breasts. Maria also witnessed sexual behaviour between her mother and Ian. Throughout her childhood and adolescence, Maria's mother, a heavy drug user, verbally abused her, and neglected her emotionally and physically, blaming her for everything. Maria's mother asked her to leave home at the age of sixteen, leading to further feelings of rejection for Maria.

Trauma symptoms and DSM criteria

According to Connor and Higgins (2008), Maria satisfied the earlier version of the DSM, namely, DSM-IV-TR for a diagnosis of PTSD and her symptoms were reported to be at a mild to moderate level. Maria identified many symptoms commonly associated with PTSD: five symptoms from Category A (re-experiencing), one in category B (avoidance) and three in category C (arousal). Maria also reported a great deal of self-doubt and lack of self-confidence. She struggled to believe she was intelligent as she failed to receive any positive feedback or praise growing up. She reported feelings of self-blame, guilt and had considerable difficulty modulating her anger. About five years ago, Maria experienced depression and panic attacks. At times she would have dissociative episodes, in which she would become dizzy, weak and collapse on the floor. She had difficulties in her interpersonal relationships and experienced sexual dysfunction with her past and current partners.

As for Mike, using the DSM-IV-TR, his symptoms also satisfied the criteria for PTSD: four symptoms from Category A (re-experiencing), three in category B (avoidance) and three in category C (arousal). He re-experienced the trauma via flashbacks and nightmares and used avoidance strategies by withdrawing from the world and refusing to admit he had difficulties. He struggled with debilitating anxiety and high levels of irritability that would culminate in him shouting at his wife and children.

Mike experienced concentration problems and felt as if he was 'losing his mind'. When he tried to tell the psychiatrist what he was going through, he kept crying, unable to articulate what happened. Mick's functioning prior to his development of PTSD symptoms was at a high level.

PTSD in earlier editions of the DSM

PTSD has had a controversial history. The impact of traumatic events began to be understood in the mid-nineteenth century when psychiatrists observed symptoms among combat veterans that were described as 'shell shock' and 'combat fatigue' (van der Kolk, 2007). These syndromes incorporated many of the current PTSD symptoms. In DSM-I, an ill-defined diagnosis, 'gross stress reaction', included war veterans, ex-prisoners, rape victims and Holocaust survivors (Friedman, Resnik, Bryant, & Brewin, 2011). However, the diagnosis was eliminated in DSM-II as it was considered a temporary condition, thus leaving practitioners with no diagnostic option for persistent conditions that resulted as a consequence of catastrophic events. 'Situational Reaction' was the only diagnostic alternative (Friedman et al., 2011). It should also be noted that, despite not being included in DSM-II, a number of syndromes were described in the professional literature around the 1970s. They were aptly named after the traumatic event itself: rape trauma syndrome, post-Vietnam syndrome, prisoner-of-war syndrome, concentration camp syndrome, battered wife syndrome, child abuse syndrome, etc.

By the mid- to late-1970s there arose a need for a new diagnosis for individuals who had been exposed to traumatic or catastrophic experiences and whose symptoms were severe, chronic and often irreversible (Friedman et al., 2011). The DSM-III committee posited that all these discrete syndromes named after traumatic events could be categorised within a new formulation of the PTSD diagnostic criteria (Friedman et al., 2011). In the DSM-III the number of possible symptoms increased from twelve to seventeen and the three-symptom clusters of re-experiencing, numbing and miscellaneous were rearranged to re-experiencing, avoidance/numbing and hyperarousal. Exposure to overwhelming or extreme stress has been retained as a precedence to the onset of clinically significant and persistent alterations in behaviour, cognition and affect.

People differ with regard to risk of persistent PTSD symptoms. The normal acute reactions to extreme stress appear not to correct themselves over time and could be seen as a failure of adaptation. It is the persistence of these symptoms that characterises PTSD (Friedman et al., 2011). PTSD remained in the revised editions of the subsequent DSM-IV. The fifth edition of the Diagnostic Statistical Manual (DSM 5) was published in 2013 with some significant changes in relation to PTSD.

According to Friedman (2013), the American Psychological Association (APA) subgroup adopted a very conservative approach as making any change to diagnostic criteria had significant clinical and scientific consequences. (See Friedman, 2013, for a detailed account of the five-year process that lead to the development of the DSM-V PTSD criteria). Most significantly, trauma and stress-related disorders were removed from the Anxiety Disorders chapter and given a separate diagnostic chapter, entitled Trauma and Stress-Related Disorders. All diagnoses within this chapter stipulate that the onset or worsening of symptoms are preceded by exposure to an adverse event. In the case of acute stress disorder and PTSD, the events must be traumatic (Friedman, 2013). It was initially proposed that dissociative disorders occupy this chapter, however none of the dissociative disorders stipulates that symptom onset be preceded by a traumatic event and there is mixed evidence regarding the relationship between trauma exposure and the onset of dissociative disorders (as seen in Friedman, 2013).

The DSM 5 criteria have remained quite broad by stipulating a twenty-symptom criterion for PTSD. (See Table 2.1 for a listing of the DSM 5 diagnostic criteria.) An important consideration in the revision of the PTSD criteria (as explained by Friedman, (2013), is that while exposure to a traumatic event is a necessary condition for the development of PTSD, it doesn't follow that most individuals exposed to a traumatic event will develop the disorder. There was serious consideration to dropping the A1 criterion, but as exposure to a traumatic event was considered a crucial part of the PTSD construct, it remained. In the DSM-IV it was not enough to have met A1 but also the individual must have reacted with 'fear, helplessness and horror' (American Psychiatric Association, 2001, p. 467). Many individuals do not experience such an intense emotional reaction and so the A2 criterion was removed as it does not predict individuals at risk to develop PTSD, nor does it reduce the number of A1-exposed individuals who subsequently develop PTSD (Friedman, 2013). A four-factor rather than the three-factor structure as seen in DSM-IV has been adopted: intrusion (B), avoidance (C) negative cognitions and mood (D) and arousal and reactivity (E). The specifier of delayed-expression has been added together with two dissociative subtypes that met the high threshold for evidence supporting their inclusion: depersonalisation and derealisation (Friedman, 2013).

The complex PTSD (C-PTSD) / DESNOS controversy

Trauma experts remain divided regarding whether complex PTSD is a distinct diagnosis and the DSM 5 appears not to resolve that issue (Herman, 1992, 2012; Resick et al., 2012; van der Kolk, 2005).

Table 2.1: PTSD criteria in DSM 5

Posttraumatic Stress Disorder

Note: The following criteria apply to adults, adolescents, and children older than 6 years.

A. Exposure to actual or threatened death, serious injury, or sexual violence in one (or more) of the following ways:

1. Directly experiencing the traumatic event(s).

2. Witnessing, in person, the event(s) as it occurred to others.

3. Learning that the traumatic event(s) occurred to a close family member or close friend. In cases of actual or threatened death of a family member or friend, the event(s) must have been violent or accidental.

4. Experiencing repeated or extreme exposure to aversive details of the traumatic event(s) (e.g., first responders collecting human remains; police officers repeatedly exposed to details of child abuse).

   Note: Criterion A4 does not apply to exposure through electronic media, television, movies, or pictures, unless this exposure is work related.

B. Presence of one (or more) of the following intrusion symptoms associated with the traumatic event(s), beginning after the traumatic event(s) occurred:

1. Recurrent, involuntary, and intrusive distressing memories of the traumatic event(s).

   Note: In children older than 6 years, repetitive play may occur in which themes or aspects of the traumatic event(s) are expressed.

2. Recurrent distressing dreams in which the content and/or affect of the dream are related to the traumatic event(s).

   Note: In children, there may be frightening dreams without recognizable content.

3. Dissociative reactions (e.g., flashbacks) in which the individual feels or acts as if the traumatic event(s) were recurring. (Such reactions may occur on a continuum, with the most extreme expression being a complete loss of awareness of present surroundings.)

   Note: In children, trauma-specific re-enactment may occur in play.

4. Intense or prolonged psychological distress at exposure to internal or external cues that symbolize or resemble an aspect of the traumatic event(s).

5. Marked physiological reactions to internal or external cues that symbolize or resemble an aspect of the traumatic event(s).

continued over page ...

C. Persistent avoidance of stimuli associated with the traumatic event(s), beginning after the traumatic event(s) occurred, as evidenced by one or both of the following:

1. Avoidance of or efforts to avoid distressing memories, thoughts, or feelings about or closely associated with the traumatic event(s).

2. Avoidance of or efforts to avoid external reminders (people, places, conversations, activities, objects, situations) that arouse distressing memories, thoughts, or feelings about or closely associated with the traumatic event(s).

D. Negative alterations in cognitions and mood associated with the traumatic event(s), beginning or worsening after the traumatic event(s) occurred, as evidenced by two (or more) of the following:

1. Inability to remember an important aspect of the traumatic event(s) (typically due to dissociative amnesia and not to other factors such as head injury, alcohol, or drugs).

2. Persistent and exaggerated negative beliefs or expectations about oneself, others, or the world (e.g., "I am bad," "No one can be trusted," "The world is completely dangerous," "My whole nervous system is permanently ruined").

3. Persistent, distorted cognitions about the cause or consequences of the traumatic event(s) that lead the individual to blame himself/herself or others.

4. Persistent negative emotional state (e.g., fear, horror, anger, guilt, or shame).

5. Markedly diminished interest or participation in significant activities.

6. Feelings of detachment or estrangement from others.

7. Persistent inability to experience positive emotions (e.g., inability to experience happiness, satisfaction, or loving feelings).

E. Marked alterations in arousal and reactivity associated with the traumatic event(s), beginning or worsening after the traumatic event(s) occurred, as evidenced by two (or more) of the following:

1. Irritable behaviour and angry outbursts (with little or no provocation) typically expressed as verbal or physical aggression toward people or objects.

2. Reckless or self-destructive behaviour.

3. Hypervigilance.

4. Exaggerated startle response.

5. Problems with concentration.

6. Sleep disturbance (e.g., difficulty falling or staying asleep or restless sleep).

F. Duration of the disturbance (Criteria B, C, D, and E) is more than 1 month.

continued over page ...

G. The disturbance causes clinically significant distress or impairment in social, occupational, or other important areas of functioning.

H. The disturbance is not attributable to the physiological effects of a substance (e.g., medication, alcohol) or another medical condition.

Specify whether:

With dissociative symptoms: The individual's symptoms meet the criteria for posttraumatic stress disorder, and in addition, in response to the stressor, the individual experiences persistent or recurrent symptoms of either of the following:

1. **Depersonalisation**: Persistent or recurrent experiences of feeling detached from, and as if one were an outside observer of, one's mental processes or body (e.g., feeling as though one were in a dream; feeling a sense of unreality of self or body or of time moving slowly).

2. **Derealisation**: Persistent or recurrent experiences of unreality of surroundings (e.g., the world around the individual is experienced as unreal, dreamlike, distant, or distorted).

Note: To use this subtype, the dissociative symptoms must not be attributable to the physiological effects of a substance (e.g., blackouts, behaviour during alcohol intoxication) or another medical condition (e.g., complex partial seizures).

Specify if:

With delayed expression: If the full diagnostic criteria are not met until at least 6 months after the event (although the onset and expression of some symptoms may be immediate).

C-PTSD, or disorder of extreme stress not otherwise specified (DESNOS) was proposed initially by Judith Herman (1992) to provide a parsimonious diagnostic niche for individuals exposed to protracted traumatic exposure — and whose most debilitating symptoms are different from the DSM-III and DSM-IV criteria. Herman (1992) identified three broad areas of disturbance that transcend simple PTSD. Firstly, the symptom picture seems to be more complex, diffuse and tenacious. Secondly, survivors of prolonged abuse develop characteristic personality changes, including deformations of relatedness and identity. Thirdly, survivors have a vulnerability to repeated harm, both self-inflicted and at the hands of others. Repetitive trauma appears to amplify and generalise the physiologic symptoms of PTSD and is charactered by hypervigilance, anxiety and agitation without any baseline state of calmness. Externalising behaviour difficulties — such as emotion deregulation, cognitive challenges, dissociation, interpersonal problems and somatisation — dominate the symptom picture. Herman (1992) argued for the expansion of the concept of PTSD to include a spectrum of disorders, ranging from brief, self-limited stress reaction to single acute trauma; though simple PTSD; to the complex disorder of DESNOS/C-PTSD that follows upon prolonged exposure to repeated trauma.

DESNOS was not included in the DSM-IV, as field trials indicated that nearly everyone who met DESNOS criteria also meets criteria for PTSD, and very little research designed to establish construct validity of DESNOS had been conducted (Friedman, 2013). However, some DESNOS symptoms have been included in DSM-V criteria, especially in clusters D and E. Inclusion of the dissociative subtype provides more scope to consider C-PTSD/DESNOS. Friedman (2013) suggests that while more research is necessary, the DSM-V criteria provides a better understanding of what research is needed.

A special edition of the *Journal of Traumatic Stress* in 2012 devoted a section to the controversy. Resick et al. (2012) reviewed the current literature on C-PTSD and concluded that available evidence did not support a new diagnostic category and suggested further research. The review indicated significant overlap between C-PTSD, PTSD, borderline personality disorder and major depressive disorder. The authors propose a dimensional structure for C-PTSD that would be more consistent with growing evidence. A more uniform definition is required, as well as the development of measures that reliably and validly assess the severity of symptoms. Goodman (2012) agrees with the dimensional approach, stating that reconceptualising PTSD along a spectrum with simple and complex features is integrative and useful. Bryant (2012) acknowledges that of course there is a symptom overlap because C-PTSD requires PTSD to be present; it is a complex variant of PTSD. He also concedes that while emotion dysregulation is a distinguishing feature of C-PTSD, a more standardised definition is required. A response by Lindauer (2012) states that a clear explanation has been provided by van der Kolk and colleagues. Lindauer states that trauma-specific treatment may not be suitable and that at times clients may be so destabilised that it would be difficult to speak about their trauma. Stabilisation versus immediate trauma therapy is mentioned, and Babette

Rothschild (2000) refers to two phases of trauma treatment where quality of life is paramount and trauma processing is secondary.

Judith Herman (2012) comments that the Resick review wasn't even-handed or comprehensive. She states that it reads like a position paper ready to rebuff arguments as to why C-PTSD wasn't included in the DSM-V. Herman posits that there is a high prevalence of C-PTSD and it is now generally recognised that the majority of trauma clients are traumatised in multiple ways. She further states that it has been well documented that C-PTSD symptoms account for much of the functional impairment in survivors of prolonged and repeated trauma, above and beyond the impairments attributable to PTSD alone. Treatments proven to be effective for PTSD alone may be inadequate or possibly even harmful for C-PTSD. Herman refers to a study by Cloitre, Miranda, Stovall-McClough, and Han (2005) that provides strong evidence for a staged treatment — one that addresses C-PTSD symptoms of affect regulation and interpersonal problems before engaging in trauma-focused exposure. This proves more effective than either component separately. The results of that study would suggest that recognition of C-PTSD as a distinct entity leads to clinically significant advances in effective treatment. Herman would like to see recognition of C-PTSD as a discrete entity, within a spectrum of post-traumatic disorders, one which would likely expand research, offer a more precise descriptive definition, as well as reliable and well-validated measures and, the development of more gold-standard treatments.

Friedman (2013) wants acknowledgement for the changes that have occurred in DSM-V and that the new criteria provide a way forward that may lead to an eventual resolution. Finally, Friedman et al. (2011) highlight the need for research investigating the question of whether protracted exposure to trauma, especially during developmentally sensitive periods, leads to a different pattern of symptoms than those included in PTSD. It also would be useful in clarifying the relationships between traumatic exposure and borderline personality disorder and dissociative disorders. Recent conceptualisations recognise that the more complex cases of PTSD involve deficits in regulating emotional distress, which are more difficult to treat because they involve acting out, self-harm, and self-destructive relationships and behaviours.

Conclusion

While Mike and Maria share a diagnosis of PTSD, the aetiology of their conditions are vastly different, and the manifestation and implications of their overlapping symptoms are very different.

Mike has a family and had a successful career. His prognosis is likely to be good and a return to premorbid functioning very likely. Maria has disengaged from her abusive family but still has relational and intimacy issues with her partner. Her self-confidence and esteem issues have improved as a result of therapy that focused on self-esteem. While there were reductions in a number of major symptom areas, the presence of three new symptoms was noted at her post-treatment interview: 'permanent damage'; 'nobody can understand'; and 'inability to trust'. Maria engaged in C-PTSD-focused therapy, which focused on symptoms such as alterations in affect modulation, self-concept, relations with others, consciousness and systems of meaning. The aim was to increase her capacity for future exploration and the working through of her early abuse.

In the words of van der Kolk (2005), 'the diagnosis of PTSD is not developmentally sensitive and doesn't adequately describe the effect of exposure to childhood trauma on the developing child' (p. 405). As a result, C-PTSD needs to be identified as a discrete entity, within the dimension of post-traumatic disorders. This would enable more clarity for those working in the trauma field to offer more appropriate treatment designed to truly support individuals with complex trauma histories and presentations.

Chapter 3

Ten things to know about emotions

There is growing research that emphasises the central role that emotions have in organising how we feel, think and behave. Adaptive emotional functioning is fundamental to our lives. When individuals seek counselling and support, they often cannot access the poignancy, significance and utility of their emotions. While there is a growing understanding of the importance and need to foster emotional awareness and emotional intelligence, there also continues to be many challenges. This chapter seeks to provide a better understanding of what emotions are, how they work and, importantly, when they are helpful or unhelpful.

1. Why focus on emotions?

Emotions play an important role in how we feel in our environment. They tell us whether important goals, values and needs are being hindered or advanced by a situation.

But not all emotions are the same. As will be described in more detail later, ideally emotions are adaptive and helpful, for example, by providing direction about how to fix problems. However, other emotions can be maladaptive, getting stuck or suppressed. They are unable to provide us with guidance, but they may also cause us significant distress (Elliott, Watson, Goldman, & Greenberg, 2004; Greenberg, Rice, & Elliott, 1993).

Our attitudes toward emotion often reflect the views of significant others: 'Just sweep things under the carpet' or 'Don't cry, suck it up.' They can also be shaped by formative experiences, such as a child watching an argument at home getting out of control and learning that anger should be avoided at all costs. There are also numerous cultural and social messages that also contribute to how emotions are viewed. These might include: 'We don't show emotion' or 'Emotions are a sign of weakness' or 'Emotions are only irrational reactions' or the idea that certain emotions are only appropriate for men, and others just for women. Sometimes we get overwhelmed by our emotions and believe that if we give into our emotions then we'll be an out of control wreck.

2. Not all emotions are equal: There are different families of emotions

There are seven Primary Emotions

Seven basic or universal emotions have been identified as universal across culture and language (Ekman, 1972; Izard, 1977). They are:

- happiness or joy
- anger
- sadness
- fear
- disgust
- interest, surprise, or curiosity
- shame

William James (1884) stated emotions are vivid mental feeling experiences of visceral changes brought about by the perception of an object in the world. Carroll Izard (2010) wrote that the most common features of emotions are neural circuits, response systems and a feeling state/process that motivates and organises cognition and action.

When we view emotions from an evolutionary perspective, we can see they were crucial for survival. Our ancestors would stand and fight or run from wild animals or invading tribes. We also see this in the animal world. A dog, for example, shows fear and shame when they cower from an abusive owner. Food that is contaminated or spoiled has an offensive odour which is shied away from, often with an expression of disgust on their face. A happy dog has smiley eyes and wags their tail. A sad one looks lost, may wail and drop their head. An interested and curious dog may search to expand their territory.

In the human world, each primary emotion has a facial expression, and this is seen across cultures and races (Ekman, 1972; Izard, 1977). It is often straightforward to identify when a person is angry by the expression on their face and the way he holds his body. A sad person may look forlorn, produce tears or withdraw. A fearful person may become agitated and it is easy to see by the expression on their face that they are scared. A person feeling shame may lower his head, show embarrassment with a reddened face and shy away. A curious person shows eagerness and interest in her surroundings.

Of course, there are many emotions or feelings but these seven are con-sidered primary in that they cannot be reduced further and because of the information they provide. Primary emotion is hard-wired in our brain stem and tied to information processing that helps a person adapt and survive by helping them to select and respond quickly to information that would take too long to process without an emotional action tendency. Therefore, a primary emotion is the emotion that a person might feel first when con-fronted with a particular situation, or might be suppressed it if it was unsafe to express it (Elliott, Watson, et al., 2004).

It is from these primary emotions that complex emotions evolve. Thus, most of the more complex emotional expressions are combinations of the primary ones and often are complicated with cognitions. For example, guilt can be a combination of anger, disgust and shame along with cognitive components. Love could be seen as a combination of joy and interest but can at times involve sadness, fear and shame. Emotions therefore, consist of a complex synthesis of elements including physical sensations, motivation in the form of needs that influence goal setting and cognitions in the form of appraisals.

Emotions are a primary signalling system (Elliott, Watson et al., 2004). In other words, when you walk along a bush track and detect something moving out of the corner of your eye, you might immediately respond with fear and freeze, or run, long before your meaning-making cognition tells you that it is merely leaves or branches rustling in the wind and not a snake. This signalling system is called neurological primacy, which is often outside of awareness. Emotions are also developed long before language and therefore precede language-based knowing. As we develop with age, emotions become fused with cognition. So, in future, the memory of that experience of detecting something moving as you walk along the bush track is blended with thoughts about whether it is indeed a snake or leaves and whether you should freeze or flee.

Emotions have the unique quality of being the interface between body and mind. They influence the biological and neurochemical aspects of system functioning and operate at the levels of the psychological, the cognitive and the behavioural (Elliott, Watson, et al., 2004).

Adaptive primary emotions have particular qualities

Adaptive primary emotions are immediate when experienced or felt. They are quick to arrive and fast to leave, they have a clear value to survival and well-being, and are the primary source of emotional intelligence (Elliott, Watson, et al., 2004). Adaptive primary emotions give people critical information about their physical and social environment at a given moment. They then prepare us for action by providing 'stick' or 'carrot' type motivation. Primary adaptive emotions integrate experience by giving meaning, value and direction. They also involve wishes, needs and wants. There is often a bodily felt sense of feeling with an emotion. Examples of adaptive primary emotions are fear at threat, sadness at loss, and anger at violation.

Adaptive primary emotions have an action tendency

The normal function of emotion is to rapidly process complex situational information to provide feedback to the person about her reaction and prepare her to take effective action. Each primary emotion has one or more associated action tendencies (see Table 3.1). Anger, when used adaptively

Table 3.1: Adaptive primary emotions and their action tendencies

Emotional expression	Description
Biologically adaptive *primary* affective responses	Provide adaptive action tendencies to help organise appropriate behaviour: • Anger at violation mobilises fight and defence of one's boundaries → *empowerment and assertiveness* • Sadness at loss mobilises reparative grief by either seeking comfort or withdrawal in order to conserve one's resources → *adaptive grieving, withdrawal and/or reach out for connection* • Fear in response to danger mobilises flight, or possibly freezing → *adaptive escape* • Disgust organises one to evacuate or withdraw from some noxious experience — *often seen in childhood sexual abuse* • Shame organises one to hide or withdraw from the scrutiny of others — *antidoted by compassion for self and/or adaptive anger* • Joy mobilises satisfaction, creativity and happiness — *feels good* • Surprise or interest — *stimulates curiosity, engagement and facilitates openness to further exploration.*

Source: Greenberg & Safran (1989, p. 25); Paivio & Pascual-Leone (2010, p. 137)

and appropriately, provides assertiveness and fosters empowerment when the individual is threatened. Sadness is required for adaptive grieving when there has been loss. We withdraw to heal or reach out for comfort. When we experience primary adaptive fear, it enables us to prepare for action in response to danger where flight or fight becomes possible. Shame signals us that we have acted inappropriately and are at risk of being judged or rejected. It therefore motivates us to make corrections to our behaviour or hide as a way of protecting our social standing and relationships. Happiness makes us feel good, and surprise fosters interest and engagement.

3. Emotions aren't always helpful

Emotions can be thought of in different ways. They can be adaptive or mal-adaptive (see Table 3.2). I have discussed how primary emotions can be

Table 3.2: Categories of maladaptive emotional experience

Emotional expression	Description
Learned *maladaptive primary* responses to the environment	Can be learned as a function of trauma or strongly negative environmental contingencies in childhood. Accessed in therapy for modification and restructuring: • Fear in reaction to harmless stimuli • Anger in response to caring and kindness.
Secondary reactive emotional responses	Often problematic and part of presenting problem. Secondary to some underlying, more primary generating process. Reactions to the thwarting of primary responses. Not often the direct response to the environment. Defensive or reactive processes. Usually bypassed in therapy or explored to access underlying processes. Readily available to awareness: • Crying in frustration when angry • Expressing anger when afraid.
Instrumental emotional responses	Emotional behavioural patterns learnt to influence people. Emotions that are expressed in order to achieve some intended effect. Explored, confronted, or interpreted in therapy: • Crying to evoke sympathy • Expressing anger in order to dominate.

Source: Greenberg & Safran (1989, p. 25); Elliott, Watson et al. (2004); Paivio & Pascual-Leone (2010, p. 137)

adaptive but what happens when the emotion system is malfunctioning? As a result of suppressing, ignoring, dismissing our emotions or having experienced trauma or neglect, we do not manage to engage and process our emotions as well as we might like to. There are three ways in which emotions are maladaptive or dysfunctional (Elliott, Watson, et al., 2004; Greenberg et al., 1993).

Primary maladaptive emotions are when primary emotions become exaggerated or do not dissipate. Often these are still people's most fundamental feelings but are no longer 'healthy' because they interfere with effective functioning. The person is no longer able to cope constructively. These reactions can be over-learned responses, based on previous, possibly traumatic experiences, thus failing to self-regulate. When expressed these emotions are often regretted. People often feel stuck in these emotions for months or even years. They feel old and familiar. They can have a disorganising quality, rendering the person feeling confused and overwhelmed without really understanding why.

An inappropriately angry person might become rageful, puff up and thrust forward. A person who suffers longstanding sadness might experience unresolved grief and become depressed and withdraw. Maladaptive fear responses lead to debilitating fear, anxiety and panic disorders. Maladaptive shame or humiliation causes us to hide or defer to others. Depression, anxiety, substance abuse and eating disorders are often attempts to regulate negative emotional states.

Sometimes there is a layering of emotions. These are called *secondary reactive emotions* and are reactions to, or defences against, a primary emotion or thought. These secondary emotions tend to obscure the real feeling and their expression rarely brings relief, unlike the expression of primary emotions. Some people who are submissive often cry when they are actually angry. Others who have difficulty showing fear or sadness may instead express anger.

The third type of maladaptive emotional functioning is known as *instrumental or manipulative*. In these cases, people strategically enact an emotion in order to get their needs met, or influence others, and usually, this process is automatic, without awareness. In either case the display of emotion is independent of the person's original emotional response to the situation. There is a 'showing' of emotions rather than the 'feeling' of them. Often, unfortunately referred to as 'manipulative feelings' these responses can become part of the person's personality. These emotions are expressed automatically — or sometimes consciously — to achieve a goal. For example, tears aimed to evoke the sympathy of others, or anger to intimidate or coerce. While the emotion may look authentic, the way to recognise instrumental emotions is that we often feel annoyed in the presence of someone 'showing us' their emotion. The evocation of compassion or care is absent because you may feel manipulated by the other.

4. The malfunctioning emotion system

There are two ways in which a malfunctioning emotion system may present — over-regulation and under-regulation.

Over-regulation

If a person experiences too little emotion, it might mean that he over-regulates his emotions. The head is in control of the heart. There might be:

- a fear of losing control
- difficulty in knowing what they want
- difficulty making decisions
- feelings of guilt
- feeling unentitled
- finding emotions unhelpful
- an inability to identify what they are feeling.

Some people do not have the literacy and skills to find emotions to be helpful, and so may think they are better to be controlled or avoided. But avoidance doesn't help. Avoidance denies the opportunity for a person to understand their perceptions and emotional reactions, and to benefit from learning from past experiences. It can also strengthen the emotion that was originally avoided.

Other people over-regulate or refuse to think about painful experiences and use suppression, distraction or dissociation as a way of coping. While there may be a fear of the emerging emotional experience sometimes such suppression leads to a maladaptive expression such as anxiety or rage. There is now evidence that this type of suppression even has physical consequences, such as immune system breakdown and other somatic complaints (Pennebaker, 1990).

Under-regulation

If a person experiences too much emotion, it might mean that they under-regulate their emotions. The heart is in control of the head. There might be:

- a loss of control when strong feelings come up

- emotional flooding that subsequently leads to an inability to make sense of what's happening

- feeling overwhelmed

- an inability to take in the experience

- increased vulnerability

- feeling unsafe and exposed.

Overwhelming emotions have a disorganising effect on thought and behaviour and interfere with learning, performance and social relations. Early abuse and neglect can become internalised as self-abuse or self-neglect. People who have an under-regulated emotional system will often have exaggerated emotional responses to situations in their environment or their relationships (Paivio & Pascual-Leone, 2010).

Usually people are generally one or the other. This can be determined by considering how the person responds to stressful situations. When we are not at our best we tend to revert to more primary responses. Another way to judge this is to consider how a person manages their emotions when they are in relationships. The under-regulator tends to value emotional expression and may have a volatile style of relating. The over-regulator is more likely to be the peacemaker and conflict-avoider.

It is important to note that emotional intelligence, as it is defined here, is a journey where there isn't really an arrival point. There are times of dramatic shifts, but more often there are gradual, incremental changes that build a sense of solidity over time.

5. Adaptive emotions need to be experienced

We usually use the thinking brain to problem-solve, but information regarding how and what we feel is accessible through activation of the emotional brain. Thinking and speaking about emotion often itself isn't enough. Emotions need to be felt and, as such, experienced. When this happens, people are moved by their emotions and they speak from emotion, making emotions accessible to change (Elliott, Watson, et al., 2004).

Often when people are 'in touch' with their emotions it can be witnessed, both in their non-verbal communication and in their voice. Their speech slows down, becoming hesitant and halting. They appear to be grasping for something, which suggests that they are connecting with an internally felt experience or emotion, an internal referent. They become self-reflective. The person is likely to refer to more specific, concrete details and be less abstract and generalised. Their language is likely to be more evocative and possibly rich with metaphors: 'I felt like a bear stuck in a trap' or 'I'm like a second-class citizen.' This can be contrasted with speech that is spoken quickly, seeks to analyse more than express, has a focus on external details or circumstances, and is abstract and intellectual.

The reason why emotions need to be experienced is related to the different areas of the brain associated with thinking and feeling. The brain activity associated with emotions is very different from the brain phenomenon associated with thinking with its own neurophysiology and neurochemical basis. When we experience feelings, the regions of the brain associated with feelings are activated. This information then becomes available to the conscious mind for reflection and meaning-making.

It is this combination of felt experience with meaning creation that indicates that the heart and the mind are integrated. Recent research suggests that the emotional brain is far more important to decision making than was once thought. Evidence for this was found with individuals who had suffered damage to the emotional centres of their brain but limited impairment to their cognitive function. When asked to make simple choices they were unable to, as even the simplest choice requires motivation at some level (Bechara, 2004).

How do we access the feeling brain?

We need to foster an attitude of observing and acceptance rather than 'doing' to allow for emotional experience. For some, this can be very challenging. But by slowing down our thinking we reduce the likelihood of problem-solving, and by noticing what we are feeling for a moment we become able to listen to what we are feeling, and as a result be more of ourselves.

Asking 'What am I feeling right now?' can be a constructive way to start building awareness of emotional experiencing. When asking this question, we are checking in with ourselves. It is less an intellectual exercise than it is a whole-of-body process that requires awareness/attending to our bodily state and to identify the place in our bodies where we feel our feelings: generally, the throat, chest, and stomach regions of our bodies.

Research has identified that each of the primary emotions is associated with different combinations of bodily activation (LeDoux, 1996). Not only do primary emotions activate facial expressions but they also appear to generate bodily states that are distinguishable for each of the primary emotions. For example, fear is often referred to as being in the pit of the stomach, sadness as heaviness in the chest area, and happiness as expansion in the chest. Anger can be felt in the clenching of the hands, tightness in the throat and pressure in the chest. Knowing these unique combinations of bodily activation helps to discriminate each of the primary emotions and helps to build awareness of the presence of such emotions.

6. Why do we react emotionally?

Emotional reactions occur for a variety of reasons. Some are helpful and adaptive, keeping us safely out of harm's way — such as the immediate response of fear to what might be a snake — whereas some are less helpful and require exploration or transformation.

Primary adaptive emotional reactions

There are two pathways to feel emotions. The first is the fast, rough and ready way, which consists of immediate responses to situations that are less accurate but timely. These include immediate appraisals of situations for danger, and fear, disgust or pleasure that arise as immediate or gut responses. These primary adaptive responses are associated with the limbic system and allow us to respond to threats before knowing what the danger is. This has been an important survival mechanism that has its origins in our evolution as a species. The second pathway enters the cortex and, as a result, is a more detailed and accurate representation, consisting of complex internally felt experiences that include cognitions, memories and bodily felt experiences.

Secondary reactive reactions

What we often categorise as emotional reactions can sometimes actually be secondary emotions. As defined above, secondary emotions are feelings about our thoughts and feelings rather than responses to situations.

Secondary emotions often relate to other, more primary emotions that for various reasons are less easily experienced. For example, we might feel angry at feeling hurt, or become self-critical when we feel vulnerable.

Secondary emotions also lack information about what you need. In reactive anger there is sometimes a quality of being upset at someone for being made to feel something. Usually, the something else is the primary emotion. For example, a person might fly into a rage when her partner arrives home hours later than expected. The fury that is first experienced may be connected to the primary emotions of sadness or fear. Reactive anger, for example, expresses the anger and may make the listener feel punished or attacked or having wronged the speaker, or some combination thereof. It doesn't tell the listener what is really felt or what is really needed. Secondary emotions lack helpful information and an associated action tendency. Therefore, it is important to bypass the secondary emotions to discover more primary generators of emotion that lie beneath.

Maladaptive primary emotions

These emotions are often formed during a highly distressing emotional experience or situation. The greater the emotional distress, the more the experience and the situation where it occurs are likely to be stored in memory. Long after the threat of the situation has subsided, the emotional response or reaction can occur over and over when the memory is triggered. A reminder of a painful emotion or memory of the situation can be enough to stimulate an emotional reaction. For example, a response such as hiding when fearful that was once adaptive can increasingly become maladaptive when triggered again and again by cues in different environments. And this can then result in a failure to self-regulate.

Transforming maladaptive primary emotions is essential. Simply access-ing them, such as through certain kinds of therapy, usually will not trans-form old and familiar responses. Often, we are aware of these responses but merely thinking about them doesn't change how we react. Transformation occurs when an old emotional response is transformed into another, more adaptive emotion and a corresponding action tendency. This occurs by first accessing the maladaptive emotion and then replacing it with an alternative emotional response. For instance, where fear is activated, which leads to the action tendency to hide (avoidance), it is only when adaptive anger is

accessed can there be an assertive response that leads to an appropriate entitlement to self-protective strategies and boundary setting. Hence, emotions
change emotion. That is why old, stuck, bad feelings that may be chronically
accessible or entrenched can be pushed down, avoided, managed, yet
continue to be reactivated and triggered until an alternative emotional
response can be developed in their place.

7. Healthy emotional experience can be disrupted by trauma and childhood abuse

Healthy emotional development requires appropriate responses from our
caregivers and sufficient environmental support. The emotion regulation
strategies employed by our caregivers, such as holding us when we are upset
or being calm in the face of our emotional pain help us to reduce distress
but if absent can impact our emotional and behavioural development,
teaching us particular maladaptive coping strategies and methods of regulation, (Paivio & Pascual-Leone, 2010). The type of attachment style,
between our caregiver and us as infants, be it secure or insecure, plays a
meaningful role in the regulatory strategies we may learn to use (Bowlby,
1973, 1988; Cooper, Shaver, & Collins, 1998).

Sometimes the environment is far from adequate or sufficient and can,
in some instances, be harmful and disruptive to emotional development.
The environment can vary from individual cases of harm and abuse to long-
term systemic forms of neglect and abuse. The effects of trauma and childhood abuse can present significant difficulties for emotional wellbeing and
lead to emotional pain. This is due to the storage of emotional experiences
in memory. In trauma, memories of distressing situations are relived over
and over again, and so our emotion system is not functioning correctly. The
person becomes hypervigilant and feels as if the trauma is happening all the
time. They live in a state of constant fear.

8. We can learn how to make emotions work for us

When we can experience our feelings rather than just referring to them, we
gain access to emotion's adaptive information and action tendency.
Experiencing emotions helps to clarify them. We have information about
what is important to us and we are moved by our emotions to take appro-

priate action. For example, when someone feels their boundaries have been violated, they experience adaptive anger and this motivates protective actions or strategies and efforts to reassert boundaries. When someone is sad, they may withdraw or activate self-care techniques or reach out for connection. Emotions tell us whether important goals, values and needs are being hindered or advanced. Having a well-functioning emotional system means that an individual has access to this important information and can act on it in their life. Once a person knows what they are feeling and from this understand what they need, they can seek to get those needs met.

Primary emotions have the quality of drawing people closer. They let other people 'see' you, while secondary or reactive emotions have the opposite effect and tend to push people away or hold them at bay. Instrumental emotions can make people feel manipulated.

Emotions can work for us when a person asks for what they need in a way that others can hear and respond to. Having emotions responded to helps to validate them and this is likely to strengthen their productive use.

Emotions are *energy in motion*. We feel stuck when our emotions are malfunctioning or maladaptive. There is no movement. Primary adaptive emotions rise in intensity and then dissipate quickly, like riding a wave. Think about watching a sad film. If our emotion system is functioning well, we will feel the cascade of emotions rising and falling. We can move quickly from sadness to happiness or from anger to fear. This idea that emotions are movements and expressions of energy helps us to recognise that emotions play a central role in motivation. It gives us a raw foundation for understanding emotions as the very thing that moves or motivates us. This definition also raises some interesting questions about emotions that have a direct bearing on how we come to regard our emotions and how to deal with them.

9. Emotional intelligence leads to appropriate regulation

Emotion regulation is the ability for us to tolerate, be aware of, put into words and use emotion adaptively to regulate our distress and to promote our needs and goals. Emotional intelligence is when there is a constructive relationship between our thoughts, feelings and behavioural responses, while adaptive functioning involves our head and heart working together.

The role of cognition in the processing of emotion is to help make sense of the emotion and then consciously and deliberately respond rather than react to it.

Two fundamental systems determine experience. One is an affective system which is pre-symbolic, and the other is a symbolic system, which is where we make meaning. The core motive of the pre-symbolic system is affect (emotion) regulation, and the core motive of the symbolic system is meaning construction. The interaction between the two systems determines experience. In other words, we have an automatic, direct, parallel system for processing of information, that is emotional (feeling) that occurs out of awareness as well as a conscious, controlled, deliberate, serial, reflexive conceptual process (thinking) that determines experience. Sometimes these two sources of experience conflict. It is quite common for our head and heart not to be in harmony. Emotional intelligence is when there is a constructive, dialectical relationship between the two sources of experience and adaptive functioning involves the head and heart working together. The role of cognition in the processing of emotion is to help make sense of the emotion or help regulate it.

To emotionally regulate is the ability to respond to the ongoing demands of experience with the range of emotions in a manner that is socially tolerable and sufficiently flexible to permit spontaneous reactions as well as the ability to delay spontaneous responses as needed. It can also be defined as extrinsic and intrinsic processes responsible for monitoring, evaluating, and modifying emotional reactions. Emotion self-regulation belongs to the broader set of emotion-regulation processes, which includes the regulation of our feelings and the regulation of other people's feelings. Healthy emotional functioning requires us to regulate our emotions and be respectful of others.

10. Shame as a social emotion

People can feel sadness, anger, joy, etc. on their own, but shame is a painful social emotion. Shame can be adaptive and maladaptive. It can be primary or secondary. It's a core or fundamental emotion that concerns one's worth or value as a person. Shame is the painful feeling that arises when we do something dishonourable, improper, ridiculous, etc. The action tendency is to withdraw and hide. The eyes lower, the upper body shrinks and collapses.

The face blushes and the heart pounds. Primary adaptive shame assists us in protecting ourselves. We hide what is judged as improper. Children's adaptive shame pulls them back from exposing those parts that are judged as unacceptable. This promotes belonging and conformity to group standards. We experience generalised primary shame when we violate group values and standards. This is an innate painful emotional response to a specific situation.

Primary adaptive shame can be distinguished from disgust which is felt about anything viewed as offensive or dirty, including thoughts, values and people. On the other hand, guilt is a complex state that involves cognitions and learned judgment about particular actions or behaviours. It is a feeling of responsibility or remorse for some wrongdoing, whether real or imagined, and can motivate atonement for that wrongdoing. In simple terms, guilt is 'You will punish me for what I've done' whereas shame is 'You will reject me for what I've done'.

Shame can also be distinguished from contempt, which is the feeling that another person or a thing is worthless or beneath consideration. Contempt is a mixture of disgust and anger and entails rejection that is arrogant and superior — the perpetual critic in the presence of an offensive odour. Contempt is similar to disgust but pertains to people and their behaviour rather than to chemically toxic substances. There is a distinctive facial expression for contempt. Sometimes it almost looks like a lopsided smile, but if you look closely, you can see the tightness in the eyes. The upper lip curls up on one side.

Shame becomes maladaptive when a generalised primary shame about violating values and standards cannot be forgiven. People hide and disavow parts of themselves and avoid situations that could invite scorn, contempt or disgust of others. This produces withdrawal and isolation. Examples of primary maladaptive shame include social rejection directed at race, poverty, disability or gender.

Shame can present as a secondary maladaptive emotion. Feelings of unworthiness and negative thoughts can lead to self-loathing. This is more situation specific and less chronic than primary maladaptive shame. If shame is generated by self-criticism we see people harshly berate, denigrate or condemn themselves for their mistakes, flaws or shortcomings. This generates feelings of worthlessness, inferiority, damages self-esteem, and may underly depression. This can be learned in one's culture or family. If the shame is generated by internal experience it can coexist with anxiety in a complex sequence of feelings and cognitions. Consequently, there is shame about feeling hurt, weak, needy, sexual or angry and feeling fearful that these internal experiences will emerge.

Shame can also exist as a core sense of self, generated by self-critical cognitions. Here, contempt and disgust are directed at the self. A sense of worthlessness or of being unacceptably flawed pervades the person. Shame is internalised through child-rearing and early shaming experiences. Stereotypically, boys being weak or girls being assertive can generate shame. People who have been emotionally, physically or sexually abused as children have internalised a sense of themselves as dirty, unlovable or worthless. They learn to treat themselves in the ways significant others treated them. They feel that they are responsible for a shameful act of which they have no control (sexual abuse) or somehow deserved the abuse and bought it on themselves. There is an inability to accept or forgive themselves, and this can result in chronic depression, anxiety and increased maladaptive avoidant behaviour (e.g. substance abuse).

Transformation of shame is dependent on the therapeutic relationship and ever-present empathic affirmation. It may be useful for the person to fully experience the shame, humiliation and embarrassment in session rather than avoid it. The experience of being seen, heard and accepted is highly affirming and can alleviate the shame. Self-compassion is then internalised to soothe the self and antidote the shame.

As you can see emotions are fundamental to our adaptive functioning. They tell us what is important and whether things are going our way. They are an efficient, automatic signalling system that is necessary for survival. They prepare us for action and give valuable information about our needs. Our emotions integrate experience by providing meaning, value and direction. Adaptive emotions lead to adaptive action.

Chapter 4

The highly sensitive person phenomena

Many years ago, I came across a phenomenon that significantly changed my life. A research clinical psychologist, Elaine Aron, conducted a PhD on what she referred to as the 'Highly Sensitive Person' (HSP; Aron, 1996). What she had recognised was there was a proportion of the population that processed information differently from others. They felt things more acutely, were highly attuned to their environment, and were often described as 'sensitive', with an acute awareness of others.

I would like to share with you my personal experiences about this phenomenon. In Melbourne, we have an extraordinarily large shopping centre called Chadstone. There are hundreds of brightly lit shops with dazzling clothes, loud music and, at busy times, thousands of people. There are many of these shopping centres in major cities around the world. I could never understand why so many people could enjoy spending long hours in such a place. After a couple of hours there, I would be completely exhausted, suffering with a headache, nausea and trembling.

I thought there must be something wrong with me that I could not endure such a seemingly fabulous place. My preference for shopping was to arrive early in the morning or go late at night when there were no people around. When grocery shopping in my local supermarket I knew where everything was and could do a full shop in less than thirty minutes. I was in and out as fast as I could. I never browsed. I went to the same supermarket for 25 years. I would be quite stressed if they moved items to different areas of the store, which often happened. If I did have to go to a large shopping centre I had a list and would go directly to the pre-researched location, to purchase what I needed and leave as quickly as possible.

When I was 15 years old, I obtained my first part-time job. I worked in the cosmetic department in Myer, one of the major department stores in Melbourne. My job was to spray perfume on the wrists of shoppers willing to be sprayed upon. By the end of the day I would have terrible headaches. I had to look glamorous and would have to wear heavy makeup, have my hair styled and held in place with hairspray (this was the late 70s), all of which aggravated my sensitive skin.

I also have other seemingly unrelated but peculiar traits. I have what is considered a sensitive digestive system and cannot eat spicy foods. As a child I only liked certain foods that were considered by my friends as very bland. I fail to understand the love of coffee. I could not stand the taste or the smell or the effect. If offered a cup of black tea, I dip the tea bag in once only and sip the extremely weak brew. When I don't eat regularly, I become incredibly anxious and confused. It seems my sugar levels drop and my anxiety increases. I startle easily and my friends would laugh as I would jump at loud noises. I don't like scratchy clothes and can only wear natural fibres. I was always considered sensitive and overemotional as a child. I was very gullible and didn't cope with being the brunt of jokes. I didn't fit in with everyone else and I never felt understood by anyone. I don't like horror movies. I can't watch violence on the news or any violent TV shows. My children are so used to this that they screen the movies I watch. I cry at everything, from cute puppies and sad movies to the impact of natural disasters and war on our planet and people. As a child I was very sensitive to any sort of pain and would feel completely overwhelmed. Major changes like moving house or a job would really unsettle me. When I was younger, I liked my bedroom a particular way and I was considered very organised. Even now my house has to have a certain level of order. I used to be quite resistant to change but this has modified somewhat as I have got older.

I could never cope with bright overhead lights and would prefer the more subdued lighting provided by using table lamps. I would love to go to parties and listen to live bands but the only way I could manage to stay for long periods of time was to have a few drinks of alcohol. The initial buzz from the alcohol helped me overcome my shyness and allowed me to become less inhibited. I loved to dance but I always felt self-conscious and again the use of alcohol helped me overcome the feeling of being exposed. People would even remark that they felt that I was quite extroverted.

I was significantly affected by other people's moods. If someone was angry I would notice it very quickly and move away. If my mother's mood was low this would influence me significantly and I would do things to try and cheer her up. If I was around happy people, I would immediately feel uplifted.

In my later working life, I found working in an open-plan office was a nightmare. I could not concentrate if there was too much noise. The words would swim around on the computer screen and I would feel overwhelmed and confused. I needed peace and quiet to concentrate. I would arrive really early to work when no one was around to get things done. I am the one with the large noise-reducing earphones, sitting in a faraway corner of an office. If someone is looking over my shoulder at what I am working on, I freeze. I struggle to multitask when I am too stressed. I did a placement at the Royal Children's Hospital in Melbourne and fortunately someone noticed my discomfort and put me in a storeroom to work. I was in heaven.

Things are not all bad. I am deeply moved by beauty and music. I am aware of the subtleties of my environment. I notice the freshness of the air and the clarity of the colours after the rain has fallen. As a child I was very creative and loved to paint and draw. That creativity has emerged later as a talent for renovating. I had and have wonderful dreams and hopes for the future. I think about things very deeply. I worry I will forget things and write numerous lists. I hate making mistakes and would feel deep shame if I had done the 'wrong' thing. Throughout my life I have been thirsty for knowledge and had a curious mind. I am extremely conscientious and ready to help anyone who needs it. I remember helping classmates with maths. I was somewhat entrepreneurial as a young person. I taught myself how to knit and made mittens and scarves and sold them at school.

When I ventured into studying psychology, I realised that I was not an extrovert at all. I had been socialised to be an extrovert because I somehow believed that was what was expected so I could be part of the crowd. But I was actually highly introverted. This seemed a peculiar realisation for me. Then I came across the HSP phenomenon. I filled out a questionnaire on the HSP website and was surprised to see that I had every single trait or quality that defined HSP. This helped me to put the pieces of the puzzle together. However, if you read the items listed in the questionnaire you would think that a person having all these particular qualities would seem quite neurotic or suffer from significant social anxiety. In many ways that can be quite true. But I found there are ways to manage this sensitivity. If I paid attention to recognising what I needed as a highly sensitive person, I could function extremely well. If I go to a party, I only go for a couple of hours. I ensure I get enough rest and solitary downtime. I eat simple food and I am happy to continue not to drink coffee or tea. A chai latte with soymilk became my new best friend. I do not beat myself up that I am not the life of the party any more. I actually really accept myself more as I am. This phenomenon helped me de-pathologise my sensitivity. So instead of seeing myself as someone deeply flawed and damaged, I was able to recognise that my sensitivity was actually a unique and invaluable quality. In my work as a psychologist it has enabled me to finely attune to my clients in such a way that they felt connected with, known by and safe with me. It also enabled me to connect to the minute details of a person's experience whilst they process their emotional pain. When I am running training workshops, I am acutely aware of the comfort of the participants and their emotional tone. I am always checking whether the temperature of the room is comfortable for people, whether people need to sit on the floor or need a cushion. This has been a gift despite initially feeling like it was a curse.

According to Aron (1996) this trait of high sensitivity is actually innate. It is a survival strategy that seems to value observing before acting. Children and adults with this trait are aware of the subtleties around them. It appears the brain processes information and reflects on it more deeply for those who are highly sensitive. Highly sensitive individuals are quite easily overwhelmed which is not surprisingly if you consider that you notice everything you are naturally going to be overstimulated when things are too intense, complex, chaotic, or novel for a long time. High sensitivity is not valued or well understood in our western world where extraversion is prized. Interestingly, 15% to 20% of the population are highly sensitive. There are equal numbers of males and females who are highly sensitive. There are some highly sensitive individuals who are also extroverts. In my opinion this is quite a conundrum, perhaps even a curse because as an extrovert you need people to derive your energy and sense of worth yet your sensitivity means that you cannot be around too many people for too long. It is a fine balancing act. If you look around and you wonder why not many people understand you or you feel like you do not belong take the HSP test and see if this happens to be a trait of yours. Also remember that for every 10 people that you may meet only one other maybe highly sensitive. Also, be aware that each person's sensitivity may manifest differently.

I introduce the idea of the highly sensitive person for two reasons. Firstly, because many people who are drawn to counselling and psychotherapy are often highly sensitive themselves. As I mentioned it can provide insight into other people's experiences that can enable a deeper connection. I believe this is necessary for working with people with complex developmental trauma. Highly sensitive people are great listeners. Secondly, I am of the opinion that a large number of people who suffer significantly as a result of their trauma seem to have this highly sensitive trait. They may in fact be more likely to be impacted by their trauma experiences and suffer emotional pain. I am not saying that a highly sensitive person is not as robust as a person who does not have this trait but there seems to be the potential for a deeper wounding especially when the trauma is interpersonal.

Elaine Aron has provided us with wonderful resources about being highly sensitive; you can visit her website at https://hsperson.com. She has written many books on the subject. On the website you can order books such as *The Highly Sensitive Child, The Highly Sensitive Person in the Workplace, The Highly Sensitive Person in Relationships*. You can also complete her highly sensitive person assessment tool online.

Chapter 5

Emotion Focused Therapy: An overview

With over a 30-year history in Canada, America and Europe, Emotion Focused Therapy (EFT) still feels like it is in the early stages of development in Australia. EFT is a complex model that can take a trainee up to two years to integrate fully. Despite its complexity, EFT is a very effective method for working with deep emotional pain. Personally, I find processing peoples' attachment injuries and trauma using EFT interventions not only a rewarding but also a humbling experience. Supporting people and facilitating their journey from deep emotional woundedness to wellness is truly a privilege. In this chapter I present to you a broad overview of what I see are the significant elements of the EFT model.

EFT, an experientially orientated psychotherapy, has its roots in the humanistic, client-centred, existential and Gestalt approaches, and has undergone a number of iterations since its development in the 1980s (Greenberg, Watson, & Lietaer, 1998). It emphasises the importance of two fundamental principles; firstly, that a genuine, empathic and affirming therapeutic relationship is facilitative of change in the client, and secondly that deepening the client's *experiencing* within the therapy sessions is a vital component of sustainable client change. The client's experiencing consists of the examination and representation of their internal worldviews, including feelings, perceptions, goals, values and constructs (Greenberg, Rice, & Elliott, 1993; Watson, Greenberg, & Lietaer, 1998). To this end, EFT has developed and adopted methods that stimulate or activate emotional experience within the context of the empathic facilitative relationship. Its approach views people as meaning-creating, symbolising agents, whose subjective experience is an essential aspect of their humanness.

According to Greenberg (2002), emotion is a brain-based phenomenon that is vastly different from thought. Emotion has its own neurochemical and physiological basis and is a unique language that the brain speaks. Cognitive theorists have argued that emotion is post-cognitive (e.g., Beck, 1996). However, recent research has shown that emotion precedes cognition (Le Doux, 1996; Zajonc, 2000) and makes significant and fundamental contributions to information processing. Greenberg has written extensively that emotion is foundational to the construction of a sense of self and a key determinant of self-organisation. (Elliott, Watson, Goldman, & Greenberg, 2004; Greenberg, 2011; Greenberg et al., 1993).

Greenberg described emotions as having a relational action tendency, as a process of meaning construction and a primary signalling system. The EFT model holds that it is important to focus on emotion because emotion provides the individual with information that serves as a primary motivator of behaviour (Greenberg, 2010). Further, Greenberg and Elliott (e.g., Greenberg & Paivio, 1997; Greenberg et al., 1993; Greenberg & Watson, 1998; Watson et al., 1998) have long emphasised that emotional arousal and depth of experience within a therapeutic session is essential in order to effect change in the client's affective functioning and view of themselves (also see Elliott, Watson, et al., 2004; Greenberg, 2002, 2004; Greenberg, Elliott, & Pos, 2007; Greenberg & Watson, 2006). They contend that emotional expression in conjunction with reflective processing is critical (Elliott, Greenberg, & Lietaer, 2004). Clients are helped in therapy to better identify, experience, explore, make sense of, transform and flexibly manage their emotions (Greenberg et al., 2007).

The most recent formulation of EFT is described in the manual written by Elliott, Watson, Goldman, and Greenberg (2004), entitled *Learning*

Emotion Focused Therapy: The Process Experiential Approach to Change. In addition to its core of traditional client-centred practice, attention is given to specific client statements, called *markers*, that indicate a client is struggling with a particular issue and is 'ready' to work with it (Watson et al., 1998). An EFT therapist follows the client using advanced empathy in order to track their process as well as assess whether to propose the use of more specific interventions or *tasks* (Elliott, Watson, et al., 2004). Advanced empathy is also referred to as *empathic attunement.* In psychotherapy it refers to the ability of the therapist to pick up on the nuances of a client's responses and to in turn respond in a way that accurately captures the sense of how they are feeling in a given moment. The client feels seen and heard. A therapist who is well attuned will respond with appropriate language and behaviours based on the client's emotional state. The therapist *experiences* the client. Within this attuned working alliance, the client remains the expert and the therapist is encouraged alternatively to follow the client's direction and then lead the process forward.

The interventions or tasks of EFT are intended to heighten the client's inner experiencing so that they can be more easily symbolised into awareness and processed. Tasks include experiential focusing, empty- or two-chair work, and systematic evocative unfolding. These different interventions pursue particular types of exploration suited to different types of processing difficulties and promote different types of resolutions. Some of the tasks are focused on the intrapsychic processes but some indirectly facilitate interpersonal functioning (Elliott, Watson, et al., 2004; Greenberg et al., 1993).

The approach was originally termed Process Experiential therapy (PE) by Les Greenberg, Laura Rice and Robert Elliott (1993) reflecting its roots and embodying the principles of it being a humanistic, experiential and process-focused approach. In 2007, Greenberg changed the name to Emotion Focused Therapy because the understanding of the role of emotion in human functioning and in therapy sees emotion as centrally important in the experience of self, in both adaptive and maladaptive functioning, and in therapeutic change and the change in name reflected this development.

EFT as an integrative, humanistic, process-orientated, evidence-based practice, is one of the most rigorously researched forms of humanistic practice and has been shown to be efficacious in the treatment of depression, anxiety, post-traumatic stress disorder (PTSD), complex post-traumatic stress disorder (C-PTSD) and trauma (Elliott, Greenberg, et al., 2004; Elliott, Slatick, & Urman, 2001; Paivio & Pascual-Leone, 2010). It is based on therapeutic methods designed to help people accept, express, regulate, make sense of; and, ultimately, transform difficult emotions. As an integrative approach, it works within a Rogerian person-centred framework that prioritises the working relationship between therapist and client, and it also incorporates contemporary emotion theory. In this therapeutic framework, there is a focus on corrective experiences, attention to meaning-making, and an emphasis on internal processing and bodily felt awareness (Elliott, Watson, et al., 2004; Greenberg et al., 1993).

Goals of EFT

EFT aims to assist people to restore healthy emotional functioning and functional affective regulation. Most people are completely disconnected from, what we call in EFT, their 'experiencing self'. This is the part of the self that favours trusting intuition and offers another level of knowledge. In EFT we want to assist people to change their style of processing of experiential information and enhance the ability to use language to describe their internal experience. In order to transform people's dysfunctional patterns we have to activate those old patterns or emotion schemes. We also aim to promote integration of disavowed and disassociated parts of self.

Emotion theory

Contemporary emotion theory says that emotion, at its core, is an innate and adaptive system that has evolved to help us survive and thrive. Emotions are connected to our most essential needs. They rapidly alert us to situations important to our wellbeing. They also prepare and guide us in these important situations to take action towards meeting our needs.

We know that emotion is a brain phenomenon that is vastly different from thought because it has its own neurochemical and physiological basis. The emotional brain is not capable of analytic thought or reasoning and its rapid evaluations are imprecise, so we need to attend to, and reflect on, our emotions to use this information most effectively. EFT aims to support clients as they experience, make sense of, and make decisions informed by their emotions and the important information contained therein.

The limbic system is responsible for all emotional responses. LeDoux (1996) identified two different paths for producing emotion. The first pathway, via the amygdala, is shorter and faster and sends automatic emergency signals to the brain and body and produces gut responses. The second pathway, via the neocortex (the front part of the brain), is longer and slower and produces emotion mediated by thought. In some situations, it is necessary to respond quickly but at other times better functioning requires the integration of cognition into an emotional response. Both these pathways are important for adaptive emotional functioning. Significantly, emotion makes fundamental contributions to information processing, and EFT can help clients to make this process more conscious.

EFT theory in a nutshell

Two basic principles underlie the EFT model. The first principle is to create a genuine empathic valuing relationship that is seen as curative in its own right and the second is deepening the client's experiencing in therapy. The sequence of activation, exploration, expression and reflection on emotion expression is central to EFT.

An important task of EFT is to bring emotions and their associated action tendencies into awareness. EFT practitioners differ from their more traditional client-centred counterparts in using more questions and conjectures to explore and stimulate the client's inner experience. In addition, attention is given to specific client statements or *markers* that indicate a client is struggling with a particular issue and is *ready* to work with it. The work of the EFT therapist is characterised by the recognition of these distinctive markers that inform the therapist of the need for a specific task or intervention.

The tasks of EFT are intended to heighten the client's inner *experiencing*, so that this can be more easily bought into awareness and processed consciously. Experiencing could be defined as the phenomenological description of the client's inner world. This description could include being aware at any given moment the sensations within the body. Most people are what we might refer to as 'talking heads'. Many of us are unable to describe our internal experience. For example, we may be able to recognise we feel uncomfortable when we are about to give a public presentation but not so specifically aware of the fluttering in our stomach, our rapidly beating heart and the tension in our chest.

Different EFT interventions (see Table 5.1) pursue particular types of exploration suited to different types of issues and promote different types of resolutions. Some tasks are focused on the intra-psychic processes; others indirectly facilitate interpersonal functioning. For example, an intrapsychic conflict within a person — or in Gestalt terms, a *split* — is seen as two opposing/conflictual perspectives in one person, which can be worked with using the two-chair dialogue (see Chapter 8). Evoking an emotional response can help the client to identify the impact of the events that gave rise to the emotion, to symbolise the client's relationship to the events, to discover their own needs and goals, and to recognise the action tendencies inherent in their emotional responses. This emotional activation and pro-cessing allows clients to become aware of the links between their inner expe-rience, the external world and their behaviour. Once these links are available to awareness and integrated through their emotional and rational systems, clients can reflect on them and make choices about alternative ways of acting that might enhance their adaption and growth, and facilitate their achievement of life goals.

Each task has a structure (see Table 5.2). This is one of the strengths of EFT as it clearly defines a beginning and middle and end for each process. In the past, process-type therapeutic work seems to have been very unstruc-tured and open-ended. Ensuring a clear structure provides safety for the client and a clear direction for the therapist to work within a particular time frame. A partial resolution is listed as part of the structure. It is not always possible to complete a task in a session and reaching a partial resolution is often a useful place to end a session. However, the real structural and trans-formational changes occur when a full resolution has been achieved.

Briefly, the EFT therapist tracks or follows the client's internal experi-ence as it evolves moment by moment within the session, offering process-ing proposals to guide or facilitate meaning construction. The therapist seeks active client collaboration and works in the creative tension between 'following' the client's experience and 'leading' the therapeutic process. The EFT interventions are regarded as particular ways of relating rather than technical treatments dealing with the client as an object. This marker-guided task strategy is combined with a genuinely prizing, empathic

Table 5.1: EFT markers, task/interventions and end states

Task marker	Task/Intervention	End state
Empathy-based tasks		
Problem-relevant experience (e.g., interesting, troubling, intense, puzzling)	Empathetic exploration	Clear marker or new meaning explicated
Vulnerability (painful emotion related to self)	Empathetic affirmation	Self-affirmation (feels understood, hopeful, stronger)
Relational tasks		
Beginning of therapy	Alliance formation	Productive working environment
Alliance difficulty (e.g., complaint, withdrawal, avoidance)	Alliance dialogue	Alliance repair (stronger therapeutic bond or investment in therapy, greater self-understanding)
Experiencing tasks		
Attentional focus difficulty (e.g., confused, overwhelmed, blank)	Clearing a space	Therapeutic focus, ability to work productively with experiencing
Unclear feeling (vague, external or abstract)	Experiential focusing	Symbolisation of felt-sense, feeling shift, carrying forward
Difficulties expressing feelings or avoidance	Allowing and expressing emotion	Successful, appropriate expression of emotion to therapist and others
Reprocessing tasks		
Narrative marker (internal pressure to tell difficult life stories, such as trauma)	Trauma retelling	Relief, restoration of narrative gaps
Meaning protest (life event violates cherished belief)	Meaning work	Revision of cherished belief
Problematic reaction (puzzling overreaction to specific situation)	Systematic evocative unfolding	New view of self-in-the-world functioning

continued over page ...

Enactment tasks		
Self-evaluative split (self-criticism, feelings of being torn)	Two-chair dialogue	Self-acceptance
Self-interruptive split (blocked feelings, resignation)	Two-chair enactment	Self-expression, empowerment
Unfinished business (lingering bad feeling about significant other)	Empty-chair work	Letting go of resentments and unmet needs in relation to the other, self-affirmation, understanding or holding other accountable

Source: Information derived Elliott, Watson, et al. (2004).

Table 5.2: The structure of a task

	Client	Therapist
Pre-marker	Before a therapeutic task emerges, the client gives some indication that it may be present, implicitly in the client's experiencing	Listen and empathetically explore
Marker and task initiation	Indication that client is ready and willing to work on task	Invitation to engage in task. Alliance must be strong
Evocation of difficulty	Client begins to explore and express difficulty while engaged in task	Facilitation of evocation with empathic exploration
Exploration and deepening	Process exploration — interpersonally or by conceptual and emotional interplay within the client	Once deep emotion emerges, empathic affirmation of vulnerability
Partial resolution	Emerging shift — client accesses new aspects	Encourage client to remain in experiencing space
Restructuring and scheme change	Deeper insights/understandings; 'aha' moments	Full reprocessing of unresolved issue
Full resolution	Carrying forward. How will this change be actualised?	Facilitate understanding of emerging new meaning

Source: Information derived Elliott, Greenberg et al. (2004).

working relationship to foster a shared, engaging, safe environment that enables the client to express and explore personal difficulties and emotional pain. An EFT therapist, therefore, needs to follow the client through focused responsiveness, or attunement, in order to track their process, as well as assess whether to propose the use of more specific interventions or tasks. However, the clients remain the experts and final arbitrators, and may reject the therapist's process directives to a task. The therapist is then encouraged to follow the client's direction.

Empathy as a task

A simple definition of *empathy* might be where one person understands, identifies and imaginatively enters into another person's feelings or experience. It could also be described as the ability to assume another's internal frame of reference. Empathy is an active, immediate and continuous process that has both affective and cognitive aspects. There is the presence of warm acceptance and regard for the other that includes profound interest, curiosity and presence. Being truly present involves being fully aware of the moment by directly encountering the client's experience, physically, emotionally, mentally and viscerally. The therapist is intimately engaged whilst maintaining a sense of centre and grounding within his or her self in that shared space.

In EFT, the degree of empathy might be best described as *advanced empathic attunement*, where the therapist tunes into the client's internal frame of reference. The client feels the therapist is 'empathically present' to them whilst they process their pain and/or trauma. There is a process of *resonating* with the client's experience. This conveys to client a sense of being really 'heard' and being nonjudgmentally valued.

From a therapeutic perspective, empathy is an active ingredient of change and a key process in assisting clients to develop a greater understanding of themselves. Its presence assists clients to feel safe and enables them to explore and deconstruct their worldviews and assumptions. Clients feel heard, understood and supported. Empathy promotes and enhances clients' capacity to regulate their emotions. It generates deeper and deeper appreciation for the client. Empathy is not just a therapeutic skill; it is a basic relationship process. Table 5.3 lists the ways in which empathy is used in EFT.

Table 5.3: Therapist empathic response modes

A. Simple empathy	Responses intended primarily to communicate understanding of immediate client experiencing.
Empathic reflection	Accurately represent most central, poignant or strongly felt aspect of client's message.
Empathic following	Brief responses that indicate that therapist understands what client is saying (acknowledgments and empathic repetitions).
Empathic affirmation	Offer validation, support, or sympathy when client is in emotional distress or pain.
B. Empathic exploration	Responses intended to encourage client exploration while maintaining empathic attunement.
Exploratory reflection	Simultaneously communicate empathy and stimulate client self-exploration of explicit and implicit experience, through open-edge or growth-oriented responses.
Evocative reflection	Communicate empathy while helping client to heighten or access experience, through vivid imagery, powerful language or dramatic manner.
Exploratory question	Stimulate client open-ended self-exploration.
Fit question	Encourage client to check representation of experience with actual experience.
Process observation	Nonconfrontationally describe client in-session verbal or non-verbal behaviour (usually with Exploratory Question).
Empathic conjecture	Tentative guess at immediate, implicit client experience (usually with Fit Question).
Empathic refocusing	Offer empathy to what the client is having difficulty facing, in order to invite continued exploration.

Source: Elliott, Watson, et al. (2004).

The task of developing a working alliance

In EFT the first task is to develop a safe working alliance. Such a therapeutic relationship is considered inherently curative, and the attitudes offered by Carl Rogers of empathy, unconditional positive regard and genuineness are understood as central change-producing aspects.

The working alliance serves two functions. First, it promotes growth by helping clients to understand and accept themselves. Second, it assists clients to develop trust in the therapist and in the therapeutic process so the client can engage in the often difficult work of self-exploration and active expression. The possibility of a corrective experience is also facilitated through a good working alliance. Whilst the first function is considered vital in EFT, the task-facilitative function of the working alliance is also emphasised. A safe empathic working environment is considered essential when introducing and facilitating the active interventions or tasks of EFT.

Advanced empathic attunement

Empathy makes it possible to resonate with others' positive and negative feelings. We can vicariously share the experience of the other through empathy. When presented with a client who has experienced emotional pain such as trauma, particular attention needs to be paid to setting the pace for the work. The trauma processing needs to be facilitated at a pace that the client can manage. This is optimised by being acutely attuned to the client. Figures 5.1 and 5.2 represent how the therapist and client are in a shared energetic space as they work together. The work of Lev Vygotsky helps to explain this. Vygotsky described a concept known as the *zone of proximal development.* This is 'the distance between the actual development level as determined by independent problem solving and the level of potential development as determined through problem solving under adult guidance or in collaboration with more capable peer' (Vygotsky, 1978, p. 86). In other words, the zone of proximal development is the difference between what a learner can do without help, and what they cannot do. As therapists we provide a space or zone of safety that assists our clients to be willing to go to their emotional pain that would otherwise be too painful to approach. Figure 5.1 represents a stage where this zone is partially shared.

The client arrives to therapy with potentially porous boundaries and is in global distress. The therapist ideally has strong, clear boundaries. In moments of deep connection and empathic attunement, the overlap might be quite substantial, as seen in Figure 5.2. It is important for the therapist to know when and how far to enter the client's zone whilst maintaining a sense of their own boundary and a sense of their own self. It can be likened to the concept of personal space. Some clients will not want the therapist to emotionally or psychologically enter that space. Advanced empathic attunement allows the therapist to become aware of this. At other times within the

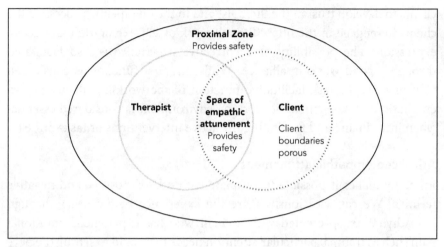

Figure 5.1
Empathic attunement creates safety.

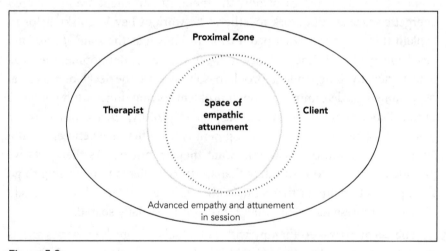

Figure 5.2
Advanced empathy or attunement at moments of deep connection.

session there may be no overlap at all. Figure 5.3 represents a state of detached presence that might be better described as *compassion* rather than empathy. Empathy is the feeling into or resonance with the other where compassion is more a feeling of concern associated with sense of feeling for the other and prosocial motivation (Singer & Klimecki, 2014). These three

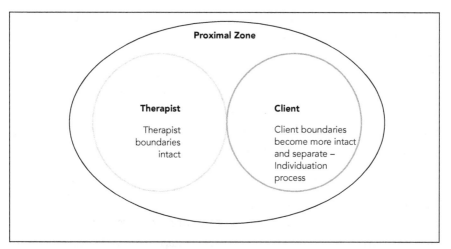

Figure 5.3
A state of detached presence that might be better described as compassion.

states may fluctuate throughout the session. At the conclusion of therapy, it is expected that the sense of self and the internal boundaries within the client are more stable and strengthened.

It's interesting to note that only empathy gets fatigued where compassion does not (Ricard, 2015). Empathic resonance can lead to emotional exhaustion and distress. Therefore, burnout could be more accurately described as 'empathy fatigue' and not 'compassion fatigue' (Ricard, 2015). Love and compassion do not get exhausted and do not contribute to weariness or feeling worn out. Compassion has been associated with positive states of mind (Ricard, 2015).

The task of systematic evocative unfolding

Systematic evocative unfolding (SEU) is especially appropriate when clients are puzzled or confused by a particular personal reaction. The marker for this *reprocessing task* is when a client describes an unexpected, puzzling, personal *problematic reaction*. The aim is to help clients bring problematic scenes alive in session with the use of vivid, concrete, colourful, and expressive language. This intervention also involves slowing the storytelling right down and incrementally retracing the events sequentially. This is intended to increase body awareness of the events. By having clients describe scenes in great detail, therapists are helping them to recall episodic memories and allowing them to re-experience their feelings of the time. In unfolding, the goal is to establish a link between a stimulus situation and the client's emotional and behavioural response to it, thus generating access to underlying emotional patterns so that they can be re-examined. Promotion of the re-experiencing of the situation and the puzzling reaction to it allows opportunity to learn the implicit meaning of the situation that, in turn, assists in making sense of the reaction. Resolution involves a new view of one's reaction in that situation.

Focusing: Gendlin's focusing style and an expanded version to process emotional pain or trauma

In 1981, the researcher and person-centred therapist Eugene Gendlin proposed that the body holds a particular kind of knowledge that could be accessed by paying attention to bodily felt sensations. He described a special kind of internal sensation, one that is a vague and hard-to-describe body awareness, as a *felt sense* (Gendlin, 1981). At this time he developed an intervention known as *Focusing* (Gendlin, 1981, 1996). Focusing involves holding an open, nonjudging attention to an internal knowing, which is directly experienced but which cannot yet be verbally articulated (Gendlin, 1981, 1996). The classic Focusing pathway, as described by Gendlin and later by Elliott, Greenberg and associates (2004), involves a sequence of finding words to symbolise the bodily felt-sense, such as a hard ball of tension in the pit of the stomach, which then ultimately culminates in an internal awareness where there is a sense of easing or a *felt shift* and a readiness to apply new awareness outside of therapy. According to Gendlin a felt shift can be a useful indicator that a resolution of the client's issue has been achieved. This may take the form of a bodily felt shift or an 'a-ha' experience. Clients often find it difficult to find words for their experiences or to make meaning of them, and symbolising this into language enhances the potential to make meaning of those experiences.

Eugene Gendlin's (1981, 1996) style of psychotherapy involved directing clients' attention to their present experience, which then influenced their physiological responses and meaning creation. Focusing involves checking words against experience and finding a *fit* that generates the feeling of certainty. Experiential focusing was developed as a way of helping clients access their experience by having them attend to their bodily felt sense.

Through the different stages of clearing the space, attending to, and symbolising their felt-sense, clients are encouraged to form a trusting relationship with themselves and their own inner experiencing. Therapists are encouraged to listen actively through attunement (advanced empathy) and to stay with the internal experience of their clients. Choosing to reflect present feeling in those inarticulate moments can assist the client to stay with, and explore, their experience rather than moving into self-analysis or criticism. Making the implicit explicit was the process goal of therapy.

Gendlin's model has a dual intention. Firstly, attending to the immediate felt-sense of experience combined with empathic understanding leads to deepening that experience. Secondly, the integration between the feeling process and the attention brought to it generates a specifiable felt-sense and symbolising it enables a carrying forward to some sort of action. The therapist's task is to carry the client's experiencing forward and to remain in touch experientially with what is occurring in their client. The skilful facilitation of process encourages exploration of the edge of the client's awareness of their experience. Deepening of that experience as it occurs in the present moment can potentially lead to new understanding and change. A full resolution manifesting as a felt-shift leads to new thoughts, meanings, awareness and feelings.

The EFT marker for the task of focusing, typically for processing an unclear felt sense, was broadened to include the reprocessing of painful or traumatic events. (This will be discussed in detail in Chapter 6.) Recent neuroscience findings have stated that reactivating a previously 'stored' memory can lead to the creation of a new version of that memory (Arntz, 2012, 2015; Lane, Ryan, Nadel, & Greenberg, 2015). This, according to Greenberg, suggests that emotion schematic memory can be changed by new emotional experience. Automatic dysfunctional emotional processes arising from traumatic childhood experiences can be altered by activating the problematic memories, generating new adaptive emotional responses, and then storing the changed memories in a stable fashion. This process is an important mechanism for understanding plasticity and potentially explaining how organisms build on prior experience while incorporating new information.

According to Greenberg, the degree to which emotional responses become disorganised and resistant to change by subsequent life experiences depends on how early they were experienced, how intensely, and how frequently they and the situations activating them occurred. In addition, the more highly aroused the emotion, the more the evoking situation is remembered. Reactivation of a long-term memory and returning it to a fragile and labile state initiates a restabilisation process termed 'reconsolidation', which allows for updating of the memory. Memories are malleable and constantly undergo revision because of the process of retrieval or recollection. When a person engages in recollection, the memory goes into an unstable state, so at that moment there is the possibility of adding information. This is not just laying down a new memory but actually changing, in fundamental ways, the original memory. Thus this *reprocessing* of the traumatic event is more than a desensitising of that traumatic experience.

It is important to note that in order to process painful or traumatic events it is essential that the client be equipped to manage it. Part of this management involves clients being grounded in their bodies and not exhibiting dissociative symptoms. *Grounding* is achieved by creating body awareness. Clients need to be confident that their flow of anxiety, emotion, memories and body sensations can be contained at will and have the ability to move in and out of distressing states. Creating a safe place is also useful as it acts as a grounding mechanism and a location the client can return to if they become overwhelmed or hyper-aroused. The expanded Focusing task will be discussed in more detail in Chapter 6.

Empty-chair task for unfinished business

A key method used in EFT is the empty-chair technique (Perls, Hefferline, & Goodman, 1951). Fritz Perls, the developer of Gestalt psychotherapy, used this simple approach to allow people to work through interpersonal conflict. It has the potential to assist people to see situations from different perspectives and to gain insight into feelings and behaviours. In EFT the adapted empty-chair task is used for unresolved issues with a significant other where the client has experienced neglect, abandonment, abuse or trauma. The representation of the other in the chair serves a function that is integral to the resolution of the dialogue. The significant other may be someone who is developmentally important. In addition, unfinished business from current relationships with partners, bosses or authority figures is often symbolically related to past unfinished business. In some trauma-related cases, unfinished business is counter-indicated especially where there is likelihood of re-traumatisation and self or other harming behaviour.

Using an empty-chair dialogue, clients activate their internal view of a significant other and experience and explore their emotional relations to the other and make sense of them. Access to unmet needs and shifts in views of both the other and self occur. Resolution involves holding the other accountable or understanding the other or forgiving the other. (More detail about how to engage in empty-chair work will be discussed in Chapter 8)

Two-chair enactment tasks

Fritz Perls was also well known for working with polarities using two-chair enactments or dialogues. Greenberg and colleagues have modified and developed the two-chair dialogue for working with a variety of internal con-flicts. Conflicting aspects of self are frequently verbalised and expressed as two parts in conflict. Such conflicts often represent internalised standards set up in the early formative years. These internalised standards, or intro-jected voices impress on the person how they 'ought' to be and interrupt the process of attending to and selecting what fits and what would lead to a greater satisfaction of needs being met. As a result, important needs get ignored, minimised or lost.

A conflict split involves an aspect of self that is coercive or critical towards another aspect of self. The critical aspect often carries hostility, disgust, or contempt that feeds into feelings of hopelessness, powerlessness, and subsequent depressive and anxious states. Various forms of conflict splits are seen in clinical depression where the negative evaluative critic evokes a need for perfectionism or emotional blocking. In anxiety disorders the critical aspect of self persistently frightens a vulnerable experiencing aspect as a maladaptive protective strategy. Conflict splits are also central to problematic substance use, eating disorders and other habit disorders. Here, conflict typically exists between a distressed, weak self-aspect that engages in persistent self-harming behaviour as a means of distracting itself from emotional pain, and a healthier aspect of the self that is concerned about the self-harm but unable to stop it. In practical terms, the two parts are put in contact by dialoguing with each other. Thoughts, feelings and needs within each part of the self are explored and communicated in a dialogue to achieve a softening of the critical voice. Resolution involves an integration between sides and self-acceptance.

It is often extremely useful to understand where critical voices are coming from. The two-chair dialogue can then become an empty-chair dialogue where significant others can be metaphorically sat in the empty chair. This allows a process where the experiencing self (often a representation of the client's child self) can express to the significant other what they needed from them and the psychological impact of not having their needs met.

A variation of the two-chair dialogue task is the self-interruptive enactment where emotional expression is blocked, suppressed or interrupted. The experiencing or healthy part of the person begins to express a primary adaptive emotion or associated need or action but is interrupted by a self-censoring part that attempts to prevent the person from doing so. Self-interruptive splits tend to be more nonverbal in nature and can have a significant bodily component of expression, such as sudden headaches or choking sensations. Self-interruptive processes are formed at key developmental stages and, generally, are responses to environments that did not allow for the full expression of emotions and needs. Although these processes are no longer adaptive, they continue into adult life and can become automated. They are learned responses designed to cope with an unsafe environment or an internalised lack of entitlement. They prevent emotional or verbal expression and experiencing.

Two-chair enactments are used to make the interrupting part of the self explicit. Clients are guided to become aware of how they interrupt and to enact the ways they do it, whether by physical act, metaphorically or verbally, so that they can experience themselves as an agent in the process of shutting down. They are then invited to react to and to challenge the interruptive part of the self. Growth in this context involves expression of the previously blocked experience.

When engaging in chair work with clients who have unresolved emotional pain due to developmental trauma, a number of key considerations need to be made. These will be discussed in more detail in Chapter 8, which discusses chair work with clients who present with a fragile sense of self as a result of developmental trauma.

Other tasks

There a number of other EFT tasks such as vulnerability, trauma and narrative retelling, alliance rupture and repair, self-contempt and compassion, emotional suffering and self-soothing. More detail about these tasks can be found in the book, *Learning Emotion Focused Therapy,* by Elliott et al. (2004). More recently, anxiety splits have been added to the suite of tasks in EFT (Watson & Greenberg, 2017).

Criticisms

There are a number of concerns related to the using of EFT with some clients. One is that emotions can sometimes have a disorganising or overwhelming effect. My answer to this is that EFT promotes the experience of adaptive emotional resources — and these are far from destructive. Another concern is that working with emotions can be painful for our clients. Therefore, an EFT therapist should be sensitive to the need for sufficient internal and external support before accessing emotions. The ability to internally sooth, as well as therapist/client dyadic emotion regulation skills, need to be in place before emotion is activated in therapy.

People who are highly rational may not respond to EFT. However, all people have emotions and need to learn how to engage in internal experiential processing and healthy emotional expression. It may take longer for such clients to feel comfortable with the emotional expression promoted in EFT. Whilst there are some limitations EFT has achieved the momentum to be recognised as an effective therapeutic approach.

Which clients are suitable for EFT?

One of the most frequently asked questions about EFT is assessing suitability for certain client groups. There is research to show that EFT is effective for depression, complex trauma, anxiety disorders, existential issues, identity confusion, gender issues, eating disorders, interpersonal issues, couples, and families. More broadly there are some key considerations that help us decide whether a client is suitable for EFT. The client needs to be able to form a good working alliance, have a certain amount of stability in their lives and be fairly high functioning.

Clients who are unsuitable for EFT are those with a high risk of suicide, who have made numerous suicide attempts or who are engaged in active or long-term drug or alcohol abuse. A person with an impulse control disorder would not be suitable. Given the emphasis on the body, someone with body dysmorphia would struggle with EFT processes. People who are actively psychotic or have with certain personality disorders – such as schizoid, schizotypal or antisocial – may not be able to engage in the experiential aspects of the therapy. EFT is not recommended for people involved in current interpersonal disputes because of the acute danger they may be in should a bolstered capacity to assert adaptive anger be actualised within their abusive relationship. Some clients with severe trauma histories with borderline traits or borderline personality and who might be dissociative need a great deal of preliminary work to be EFT-ready. The concept of dissociation and how to work with it when processing emotion pain will be discussed in Chapter 6. Other barriers for suitability include difficulties in symbolising feelings, or activating or integrating dysfunctional or conflicting emotion schemes.

Having raised these cautions, it is still possible to counsel and support such complex clients using the person-centred approach informed by the EFT principles. The main consideration is to not engage in the task work until the client is 'ready, willing and able'.

How do we formulate a case in EFT?

EFT has its own characteristic method for formulating a case. In simple terms, the formulation focuses on the working relationship and is process-orientated, tentative and ongoing, moment-by-moment. There is an emphasis on being process-dependent and not content-dependent. The EFT therapist closely tracks the client's experience and uses empathic exploration. They are guided by the *markers*, which then in turn inform the use of the different tasks.

As with most modalities it is important to develop a *focus* in therapy and this focus is the basis for the case formulation. The process diagnosis is amended continuously, co-constructed with the client and helps guide the course of therapy and interventions. There is an emphasis on descriptions of patterns of functioning rather than types of people. In line with this person-centred philosophy, EFT practitioners work to trust the internal resources of the client and work to activate the innate growth tendency towards healing that is present within most clients. There is no *plan* for a session as the markers indicate which interventions to use. The primary objective is to creatively tailor the specific interventions to the individual client.

The EFT therapist facilitates the unfolding of the narrative of the client's life story by actively listening and noticing the narrative style. For example, is the client able to be self-reflective or are they externalising and projecting? Both client and therapist work together to identify the presenting problem. The EFT therapist listens for what's poignant and painful in the narrative. The emotional and processing style is noted. What capacity does the client have to emotionally regulate? Emotion regulation is the ability to respond to the ongoing demands of life's experiences with a range of emotions that is socially tolerable and sufficiently flexible to permit spontaneous reactions as well as the ability to delay spontaneous reactions as needed. Is the client over-regulated or under-regulated? Are they conceptual or experiential? What is their depth of experiencing? What is their degree of emotional arousal? Are they dysregulated and what extent do they have emotional awareness? Another feature that is worth noting is vocal quality. Does the voice quiver with emotion or is it focused and limited or is there an external emphasis?

A significant part of the case formulation is to identify and follow the *core emotional pain*. This is understood in relation to the client's early attachment and identity histories and played out in current relationships. Then there is the *core emotion scheme*. In EFT terms, this is the underlying maladaptive behaviour pattern of the individual's core pain or core belief, such as a fear of abandonment, or a sense of worthlessness.

Individuals often struggle to feel comfortable 'in their own skin'. This is evident in how they relate to themselves intra-psychically and can be referred to as having *intra-psychic* issues within the *self-self* relationship. Interpersonal or *inter-psychic* issues can be referred to as *self-other*. Issues with how they view themselves in relation to the world are seen as existential or *self-world*. Themes of dysfunctional relationships with self, other and the world are important to identify as they assist in setting the direction for the work and help identify interventions. People may have a single predominant relationship theme or a mixture of all three.

It is imperative that therapist and client co-create a focus for the work. If, as a therapist, you have the belief that the issues that clients present with are related to unresolved childhood events and your client wants strategies on how to manage their anger or anxiety there is likely to be a rupture in the working alliance. It is important to have agreement. Such goals need to be discussed and explicitly identified. Some clients are willing to explore the underlying issues when informed that this may help with their emotion regulation and treat their underlying cause for their symptoms but they need to be informed in a way that makes sense to them and that it may take time as it is not 'a quick fix'. The therapist can co-construct the case formulation narrative with the client by linking presenting relational and behavioural difficulties to triggering events and core emotion schemes.

A key part of the formulation is the identification of the *markers*. This concept that clients indicate their readiness to work through their presenting issues by using certain language — the markers — is a very distinctive characteristic of EFT. The markers indicate which interventions or tasks are presented to the client to work through in each session. Markers are identified within each session but a meta-level perspective formulation of the marker can also be considered. A client who has ongoing issues with authority figures may in fact have unfinished business with their father. A deeply ingrained sense of perfectionism that manifests in an eating disorder may be an introjected voice of the client's mother. Many markers may present during the course of the therapy but the overarching meta-perspective marker should be held in mind by the therapist. Taking a meta-perspective in this way can provide the overall direction for the therapeutic work.

Identifying whether emotions are adaptive or maladaptive gives the therapist important information about what emotions need to be focused upon. Primary maladaptive emotions are learned as a function of trauma or strongly negative environmental contingencies in childhood. They need to be accessed in therapy for modification and restructuring. They are the appropriate emotion but have got stuck, are often of excessive intensity and are enduring. Being stuck in anger is an example. Secondary reactive emotions are often problematic and can be part of the presenting problem. These emotions are secondary to some underlying, more primary generating process. They are like triggered defensive or reactive processes that are not often the direct responses to the environment. They are usually

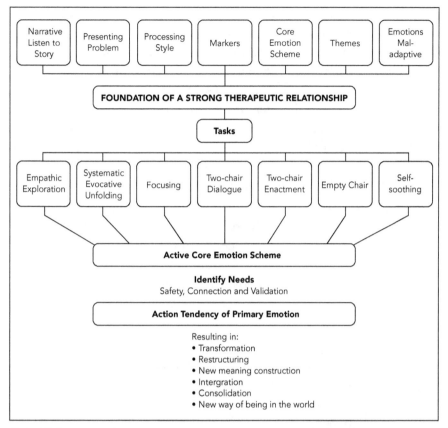

| Narrative Listen to Story | Presenting Problem | Processing Style | Markers | Core Emotion Scheme | Themes | Emotions Mal-adaptive |

FOUNDATION OF A STRONG THERAPEUTIC RELATIONSHIP

Tasks

| Empathic Exploration | Systematic Evocative Unfolding | Focusing | Two-chair Dialogue | Two-chair Enactment | Empty Chair | Self-soothing |

Active Core Emotion Scheme

Identify Needs
Safety, Connection and Validation

Action Tendency of Primary Emotion

Resulting in:
• Transformation
• Restructuring
• New meaning construction
• Intergration
• Consolidation
• New way of being in the world

Figure 5.4
Summary of EFT case formulation

bypassed in therapy or explored to access underlying processes. Instrumental or manipulative emotions are emotional behavioural patterns that have been learned to influence people. These emotions are expressed in order to achieve some intended effect. They can be explored, confronted, or interpreted in therapy. They can also become part of a person's personality and, therefore, be resistant to change. Figure 5.4 provides a diagrammatical representation of the case formulation process.

In summary, the EFT therapist needs to assess whether the client is ready, willing and able to engage in the work. The 'work' is using tasks. It is imperative to lay the foundations to work in a process-experiential emotion-focused way. The creation of external and internal safety for the client is paramount (these concepts will be discussed in detail in Chapter 6). If a client is externalising and projecting and unable to engage with their inner experience it is prudent to work at a more cognitive level, using the person-centred approach (PCA), cognitive–behaviour therapy (CBT), acceptance and commitment therapy (ACT) or motivational interviewing (MI; see Figure 5.5). If the client is able to engage in inner exploration of their experience then EFT is suitable, and restructuring, transformation, integration and consolidation is possible. Reflection on the work involves assessing how new meaning influences or fits in with the reconstruction of new narratives and connects back to presenting problems.

EFT invites people to approach, attend to, regulate, make effective use of and transform emotions. EFT also recognises the power of human relationships to heal. EFT therapists offer an opportunity for healing and transformation, through not only the genuine person-centred therapeutic relationship but also with appropriate use of the powerful EFT tasks.

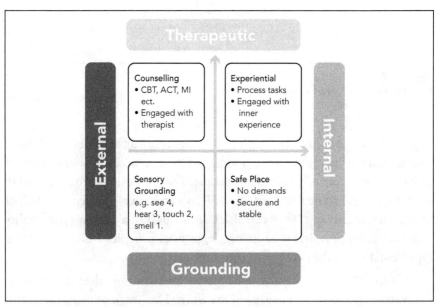

Figure 5.5
Assessing whether the client is ready, willing and able to engage in the work.
Source: Berry (2015).

Chapter 6

Development of the expanded focusing task

I would now like to tell you the story of how the expanded focusing task came about. I discovered Emotion Focused Therapy (EFT; or as I mentioned in Chapter 5, process experiential [PE] therapy as it was known as then), in my postgraduate training. I knew instinctively that human beings deep down were more than their cognitions, and here was EFT, a complex and well-researched model that focused on emotions rather than cognitions. Cognitive–behaviour therapy (CBT) was considered the gold standard evidence-based approach then and still remains so. But watching the person-centred, EFT demonstrations, I was immediately struck by the therapist's focus on the experiential process rather than on the content of a client's story. This deepened the exploration of a client's experience much more than if the client had just talked about what was happening. In these live demonstrations I saw the transformative power for people to be liberated from past trauma and emotional pain, more effectively than working purely with the person's cognitions.

During my postgraduate training I completed a doctoral dissertation study examining the effectiveness of EFT in the case studies of four young women who were clinically anxious and depressed, and who received a minimum of twelve EFT counselling sessions. Each session was video recorded and transcribed, thereby documenting the young women's entire therapeutic journey. The results of that qualitative case study investigation identified very clearly that the working relationship *and* the EFT tasks were responsible for the changes that were reported to have occurred and observed. I became very interested in what happened within each session that led to change. I watched each recording with great interest, hoping to uncover more moment-by-moment features that could be identified as change events. I had a strong conviction that unresolved or unintegrated early childhood trauma or painful events impacted a person in the present. It became clear to me that the early childhood experiences of the young women were indeed directly related to their current difficulties. In that research I began to use the focusing task with the intention to explore the early experiences of these women. While I found the classic focusing task very useful it did not quite seem enough to just connect with the felt sense and then wait for some insight or shift. This early work was the beginning of my idea to expand the focusing task to resolve emotional pain by reprocessing painful or traumatic events.

Classic focusing has been adapted within EFT, both as a task and as a subtask within other tasks, such as focusing on their internal experience whilst engaged in chair work for example (Elliott, Watson, Goldman, & Greenberg, 2004; Greenberg, Rice, & Elliott, 1993). While in EFT terms, the felt sense was redefined as a representation of an emotion scheme, the task of focusing itself was applied in the EFT model much as Gendlin had originally described it. But the model offered no suggestion about what to do when the felt sense connected to earlier painful or traumatic memory.

Primary emotions

In order to understand the potential usefulness of expanding the focusing task I need to explain the role of primary emotions (see also Chapter 3). A primary emotion is an emotion experienced as 'an immediate and direct response to the environment that is not reducible to or mediated by other cognitive-affective components' (Paivio & Pascual-Leone, 2010, p. 59). The current EFT definition of a primary adaptive emotion is a person's first, immediate response to a situation (Greenberg & Goldman, 2019). In my research (Harte, 2012, 2017), I defined a primary emotion as being an emotion that is basic, discrete, innate, quick to dissipate, and related to survival and adaption. As we discussed in Chapter 3, seven such discrete basic or primary emotions have been identified and generally accepted within the literature: fear, anger, sadness, surprise, disgust, shame, and joy (Ekman, 1972; Greenberg, et al., 1993; Izard, 1977). Such emotions have primacy and show universal characteristic facial expressions (Greenberg et al., 1993). Each primary emotion has a specific action disposition or action tendency, which refers to an urge to carry out a certain expressive behaviour (see Table 6.1). For example, the action tendency of fear involves an urge to escape, and that of anger involves an urge to attack or protect one's boundaries (Elliott, Watson, et al., 2004; Greenberg et al., 1993). The action tendency of an emotional reaction could be regarded as its essential defining characteristic. In addition to these primary emotions, Greenberg and Safran (1987, 1989) proposed that emotional experience becomes elaborated into subtle blends of emotions such as love, pride, or envy, and can be expressed in maladaptive or unproductive ways (see Table 6.1).

Emotional pain and trauma

Primary emotions are biologically adaptive responses that reflect basic human needs and promote survival-oriented action tendencies (Izard, 1977). An *emotional injury* occurs in situations where the biologically adaptive response of a primary emotion is inhibited or restricted, and the fulfilment of basic human needs to be loved, validated, and safe are prevented or violated. An injury of this kind has an enduring quality, experienced as *emotional pain,* that burdens a person long after the event has ceased. Emotional pain is the unpleasant, overwhelming, upsetting internal experience or 'response to an injury that prevents or violates the fulfilment of the basic human needs of being loved, safe and acknowledged' (Timulak, 2015, p. 2).

One powerful example of an emotional injury is trauma, such as an accident, assault, serious injury, interpersonal violence, emotional abuse, sexual abuse, or natural disaster. Officially, a post-traumatic stress disorder (PTSD) diagnosis could result after a 'large T' trauma. Examples of 'small t'

Table 6.1: Categories of emotional experience and their action tendencies

Emotional expression	Description
Biologically adaptive *primary* affective responses	Provide adaptive action tendencies to help organise appropriate behaviour: • Anger at violation mobilises fight and defence of one's boundaries → empowerment and assertiveness • Sadness at loss mobilises reparative grief by either seeking comfort or withdrawal in order to conserve one's resources → adaptive grieving • Fear in response to danger mobilises flight, fight or possibly freezing → adaptive escape • Disgust organises one to evacuate or withdraw from some noxious experience — often seen in childhood sexual abuse • Shame organises one to hide or withdraw from the scrutiny of others — antidoted by compassion for self and/or adaptive anger • Joy mobilises satisfaction, creativity and happiness — feels good • Surprise or interest — stimulates curiosity, engagement and facilitates openness to further exploration.
Learned *maladaptive primary* responses to the environment	Can be learned as a function of trauma or strongly negative environmental contingencies in childhood. Accessed in therapy for modification and restructuring: • Fear in reaction to harmless stimuli • Anger in response to caring and kindness.
Secondary reactive emotional responses	Often problematic and part of presenting problem. Secondary to some underlying, more primary generating process. Reactions to the thwarting of primary responses. Not often the direct response to the environment. Defensive or reactive processes. Usually bypassed in therapy or explored to access underlying processes. Readily available to awareness: • Crying in frustration when angry • Expressing anger when afraid.

continued over page ...

Instrumental emotional responses	Emotional behavioural patterns learnt to influence people. Emotions that are expressed in order to achieve some intended effect. Explored, confronted, or interpreted in therapy: • Crying to evoke sympathy • Expressing anger in order to dominate.

Source: Greenberg & Safran (1989, p. 25); Paivio & Pascual-Leone (2010, p. 137).

trauma include non–life-threatening injuries, emotional abuse, death of a pet, bullying or harassment, and loss of significant relationships. People have unique capacities to handle stress, which impacts their ability to cope with trauma. What is highly distressing to one person may not cause the same emotional response in someone else, so the key to understanding 'small t' trauma is to examine how it affects the individual rather than focusing on the event itself. While these instances can seriously challenge a person's ability to cope, they are typically not considered sufficient to cause mental health issues. As our understanding of trauma has advanced, it is increasingly recognised that multiple 'small t' traumas can result in a significant cumulative effect. Interestingly, the word *trauma* has been used to describe both the stressor and the reactions to the stressor (Ford, 2009). The *Diagnostic and Statistical Manual of Mental Disorders* (5th ed.; DSM-5) states that exposure to a traumatic or stressful event can result in psychological distress (American Psychiatric Association, 2013). Here I describe the stressor as the emotional injury and the reactions to the felt sense of emotional pain. I use the word *trauma* for any incident, whether it be 'small t' or 'large T' trauma events that leave the person with unresolved emotional pain.

As my interest in working with people with emotional pain and trauma expanded I was drawn to the writings of other trauma researchers. The trauma researcher Bessel van der Kolk (1995) wrote that, for some people, traumatic experiences are encoded primarily in right-brain experiential (nonverbal) memory, in the form of emotions, images and bodily sensations, and are not processed on the symbolic or verbal level, thereby leaving the experiences unintegrated. Additionally, the sympathetic nervous system can activate the fight-flight response during a trauma, thereby making the

71

integration of painful or traumatic experiences less likely (Rothschild, 2011). Activation of the autonomic nervous system can lead to freeze or dissociation at the time of the traumatic event, as explained by the polyvagal theory (Porges, 2007), and can interfere with making sense of or resolving the experience. Sometimes, these painful or traumatic experiences might be recalled only as undifferentiated emotions and body sensations.

Why is *felt sense* important?

As mentioned in Chapter 5, researcher and person-centred therapist Eugene Gendlin proposed that the body holds a particular kind of knowledge that could be accessed by paying attention to bodily felt sensations. To recap, he described this special kind of internal sensation, one that is a vague and hard-to-describe body awareness, as a *felt sense* (Gendlin, 1981) and went on to develop the intervention known as *focusing* (Gendlin, 1981, 1996). Focusing involves holding a kind of open, nonjudging attention to an internal knowing which is directly experienced but is not yet in words (Gendlin, 1981, 1996). The classic focusing pathway as described by Gendlin and later by Elliott, Greenberg and associates (2004) involves a sequence of finding words to symbolise the bodily felt sense, such as a hard ball of tension in the pit of the stomach, which then ultimately culminates in an internal awareness where there is a sense of easing or a *felt shift* and a readiness to apply new awareness outside of therapy. According to Gendlin, a felt shift can be a useful indicator that a resolution of the client's issue has been achieved. This may take the form of a bodily felt shift or an 'a-ha' experience. Clients often find it difficult to find words for their experiences or to make meaning of them, and symbolising this into language enhances the potential to make meaning of those experiences. In EFT, the task of focusing has been utilised to access internal emotional experiences. The *marker* for the task of focusing, defined as an experiential readiness to work with an issue, is typically an *unclear felt sense*.

The notion of processing painful/traumatic events within a focusing task has not been tested or documented. I questioned Les Greenberg in 2010 and Sandra Paivio in 2011 as to whether they used the focusing task to process painful or traumatic events and they responded that they did not as their focus was more on the use of chair work to process emotional pain.

As I encouraged the young women who were part of my doctoral research to *sit* with their felt sense experience, episodic memories would sometimes emerge. I realised that felt sense could be used as an access point into past memories and experiences where episodic memories were not readily available to the conscious mind. It struck me that this was a significant aspect of a change event that I had been looking for. What was exciting was the realisation that these episodic memories were memories of emotional injuries where the adaptive response to a primary emotion was thwarted. A current felt sense links the person to a memory of an old unresolved issue. Once this old emotional pain was brought into current awareness it could be worked with. I found that many unresolved issues tended to be as a result of interpersonal difficulties with significant others, particularly parents.

In EFT, the marker for unfinished business is empty-chair work but many people resist the idea of moving chairs as required in classic-chair work. I wondered whether it would be as effective to do the chair-work dialogue using imagery rather than confronting a significant other in an empty chair. This initial observation led me to construct a hypothetical model of the expanded focusing task. In my practice I used this expanded task with clients and refined aspects of it. Years later I undertook further research using task analysis to analyse the hypothetical model and build an empirically derived model of how to work with individuals who have experienced painful and traumatic events (see details of the task analysis at end of this chapter). What I present to you now are the results of that research.

Conceptual influences in the conceptual development of the extended focusing task

As EFT is an integrative model, I thought it was appropriate to incorporate concepts and philosophies from other leading theorists in the field so as to best support and facilitate clients as they work through processes of change. These included contemporary trauma theory (e.g., Rothschild, 2000), in particular, the work of Babette Rothschild (2000, 2004), which asserts that memories — including trauma memories — are stored in the body, which provides an important addition to the model. Other leading trauma therapists agree that body-orientated psychotherapy, or somatic psychotherapy, is effective for dealing with unintegrated trauma experiences (e.g., Levine, 2015; Ogden, 2006; Ogden & Fisher, 2015).

In 1987, Greenberg and Safran proposed an integrative theory of emotional processing as a framework for understanding emotional processes and change in therapy (see Greenberg & Safran, 1987, 1989). As already mentioned, primary emotions were hypothesised to be biologically adaptive responses that reflected survival needs and promoted survival oriented problem solving (Izard, 1977). As mentioned earlier there are seven specific primary emotions which were identified: fear, anger, sadness, surprise, disgust, shame and joy (Ekman, 1972). The primary emotion experienced 'is an immediate and direct response to the environment that is not reducible to or mediated by other cognitive-affective components' (Paivio & Pascual-Leone, 2010, p. 59). Each primary emotion was identified as having an action tendency (see Table 6.1). In addition to these primary emotions, Greenberg and Safran (1987, 1989) proposed that emotional experience can be expressed in maladaptive or unproductive ways (see Table 6.1).

According to this framework, primary emotions need to be accessed into conscious awareness for their adaptive information and capacity to organise action. By contrast, maladaptive emotions need to be accessed in order to be transformed, in a process that exposes them to new experience and thereby creates new meaning. Secondary emotions need to be bypassed in order to get to more primary emotions (Greenberg & Pascual-Leone, 2006). The quality of the adaptive primary emotions is quite different from maladaptive emotions. With a natural rising and falling in intensity, they feel right for the given situation and have adaptive qualities. A number of primary emotions may be experienced for any given situation.

Greenberg (2011) stated that the degree to which emotional responses become disorganised and resistant to change depends on how early they were experienced, and how intensely and frequently they occurred. In some people the more highly aroused the emotion, the more the evoking situation is remembered (McGaugh, 2000). In other people, traumatic memories are suppressed (Paivio & Pascual-Leone, 2010; Rothschild, 2000).

A very interesting phenomenon that has been identified in neuroscience really caught my attention. There is now strong research identifying that reactivation of a long-term memory returns the memory to a fragile and labile state, initiating a restabilisation process termed *reconsolidation*, which allows for updating of the memory (Hupbach, Gomez, Hardt, & Nadel, 2007; Hupbach, Hardt, Gomez, & Nadel, 2008; Lane, Ryan, Nadel, & Greenberg, 2015). Reconsolidation has been suggested as an important mechanism for understanding plasticity, potentially explaining how organisms build on prior experience while incorporating new information (Hupbach et al., 2007; Lane et al., 2015). Hupbach and associates showed that at times of reconsolidation, new input could alter the original memory, which could then be *consolidated* by incorporating new material into the old memory. Reactivating a previously stored memory can lead to the creation of a new version of that memory (Hupbach et al., 2007; Lane et al., 2015). Lane et al. (2015) proposed that change occurred by activating old memories and their associated emotions, and introducing new emotional experiences in therapy may enable new emotional elements to be incorporated into that memory trace via reconsolidation. This, according to Greenberg (2011), suggests that emotion-laden schematic memory can be changed by new emotional experience. This was very exciting to me because it suggested we could change our emotional responses to early painful and traumatic events.

Lane et al. (2015) explained that the intensity of emotion during an event, regardless of positive or negative valence, increases the likelihood that the memory will be recalled vividly and the original emotion re-experienced, including the visceral or bodily manifestations of that emotion. Activation of the hyperthymic–pituitary–adrenal (HPA) axis results in a cascade of stress hormones being released which may enhance encoding but at other times the stress hormones may actually impair the memory.

Timulak (2015) asserts that the accessed painful emotions are at the centre of problematic emotion schemes and self organisations. These painful emotions and their associated unmet needs have their origin in past or current salient emotional injuries. According to Greenberg and associates, accessing the unmet need associated with maladaptive emotions, and providing a sense of rightfully deserving to have the childhood need met creates a sense of agency (Elliott, Watson, et al., 2004; Greenberg, 2011; Pascual-Leone & Greenberg, 2007; Timulak, 2015). The corrective experience occurs within a new context, the context of therapy itself, which can also be incorporated into the old memory by the processes of reactivation, re-encoding and reconsolidation (Elliott, Watson, et al., 2004; Lane et al.,

2015). Thus, through-evoking painful memories and identifying unmet needs and *experiencing* these unmet needs as valid, memories of emotional injuries are reorganised.

An important premise in EFT is that the expressed unmet need and the action tendency associated with the accessed primary emotion lead to adaptive action (Greenberg & Watson, 2006). Contacting the fundamental need and realising the action tendency provide motivation and direction for change and an alternative way of responding. From a purely behavioural perspective, an action tendency is the operational definition of an emotion, however from an experiential perspective it is one facet of a complex experience that is laden with personal meaning (Paivio & Pascual-Leone, 2010). Timulak (2015) found that once the core primary emotions are accessed, differentiated, and stayed with, the therapist facilitates the client's focus on the unmet needs embedded in those core painful emotions. Unmet needs embedded in *shame*-based emotions include the need to be accepted, seen and validated. *Fear*-related emotions include the need for protection and safety. Needs to be loved, connected with and cared for are needs embedded in *sadness*–related emotions (Timulak, 2015).

Within the extended focusing task's episodic memory, accessing the primary emotion and the corresponding action tendency associated with that emotion leads to adaptive action tendencies that help organise appropriate behaviour. Often the fundamental need has been suppressed and emerges within the recalled memory. For example, the child accesses suppressed anger at the parent perpetrating violations, or they might experience sadness at the loss of the parent's attention and support, or fear in response to the danger of being hit or scolded.

In my opinion an ultimate aim of therapy is consolidation of traumatic memories to stabilise the event memories and render them less susceptible to interference from similar experiences, and thus more likely to be comfortably recollected at a later date (Lane et al., 2015). Bessel van der Kolk (1995) stated that being able to express traumatic emotional memories in words helps promote their assimilation into one's ongoing self narrative. Rubin, Berntsen, and Bohni (2008) proposed that PTSD symptoms do not derive from the emotional experience of the original event per se, but from the explicit memory for that event that is constructed and reconstructed through subsequent recollections. Often the unexpressed intense emotions remain associated or fused with the episodic memory.

Rossouw (2013), a neuropsychologist, discussed the idea that neural 'loops' or clusters are formed when neurons fire in a specific sequence, which in turn lead to a stronger neural connection and an upregulation of neural activity. This is based on Hebb's Law and the concept that 'neurons that fire together, wire together' (Rossouw, 2013, p.6). He presented neuro-biological evidence that new, effective neural pathways can be established using talking therapy of different modalities. The concept of 'neurons that fire apart, wire apart' was used to explain this phenomena (Rossouw, 2013, p. 7). When the new patterns are established and regularly activated, the old firing patterns not only will become less preferred patterns but will slowly start to deconstruct thus resulting in less risk of relapse into the default patterns (Rossouw, 2013). This suggests that reprocessing painful or trau-matic memories has the potential to untangle these neural clusters which will assist in reducing symptoms.

Importance of emotional arousal for change

There is good evidence that emotional arousal is an important factor for the success of many different forms of psychotherapy (see Lane et al., 2015). Greenberg and associates have shown that emotional arousal whilst engaging in imaginal exposure of the autobiographical memory is an important aspect of the mechanism of change (Greenberg, 2011; Greenberg & Watson, 2006). However, it has also been shown that too much or too little arousal when emotion is being processed is not necessarily linked to outcome (Carryer & Greenberg, 2010). Lane et al. (2015) stated that if emotional arousal is too intense, the mentalising function mediated by a neural network including the medial prefrontal cortex goes offline, limiting the capacity of reflection. In other words the flight/fight mechanism is activated and the ability to access executive cognitive functioning is reduced. Babette Rothschild (2011) explained therapeutic interventions are unlikely to be effective and integration of emerging understanding won't occur if arousal levels become too high because the flight/fight or polyvagal (freeze) systems have become activated. She describes the idea of 'putting on the brakes' as a way of managing increased arousal so that new information can be inte-grated when the client is in a low-level to moderate-level aroused state (Rothschild, 2004). However, if arousal is too low then cognitive processing of emotions, integration and meaning-making is not likely to occur. Low arousal needs to be increased to achieve sufficient emotion activation and high arousal needs to be decreased. Additionally, effective psychotherapy occurs in conditions of safety promoted by a good therapeutic alliance in which the client can rely on the therapist to facilitate experiences that are new but not overwhelming. Thus it appears that a combination of emotional arousal and reflecting on the emotion, is a better predictor of outcome than either alone (Carryer & Greenberg, 2010; Lane et al., 2015).

Numerous behaviour therapies based on exposure have been shown to be effective for the treatment of PTSD, but as Greenberg and Pascual-Leone (2006) note, research on behavioural exposure has shown that only some individuals actually engaged in this exposure task and therefore only some were able to benefit from the treatment. An alternative to behavioural exposure for the treatment of PTSD was presented by Arntz (2015) who promoted the idea of *imagery rescripting* as an effective alternative that has been recently accepted in mainstream CBT. Imagery has been used in psychotherapy for decades. The basic idea of imagery rescripting is to activate the trauma memory and imagine a different ending that better matches the needs of the client. The therapeutic effects are not based on a simple replacement of the original memory by new memory because as research by Arntz (2012) has showed, the facts of the original trauma memory are not forgotten or overridden by the rescripting.The mechanism seems to be a change in the *meaning* of the trauma memory, brought about by experiencing in the imagination of what one needed at the time and getting unmet needs met. This is a different mechanism from extinction, on which exposure treatment is based. Exposure treatment does not change the meaning of the trauma memory itself, but leads to the formation of an alternative memory trace. Expression of needs, feelings and actions which were inhibited at the time, usually for survival reasons, were considered a healing factor (Arntz, 2012; Greenberg, 2011).

Current research by Arntz (2015) has showed that imagery is a more powerful way than talking to change traumatic memories and the associated meaning and emotions. During traumatic events it is natural that all kinds of needs, emotions and action tendencies are triggered but they are usually not fully actualised. It is healthy and corrective to imagine emotions to be expressed, actions to be carried out and needs to be met. The client can imagine all kinds of changes in the rescripting that meet their needs and it is not important whether these changes are realistic. The rescripting process is done in prior sessions and then presented to the client in a subsequent session. (See Arntz, 2012, 2015). If there has been childhood abuse, one form of rescripting is asking the client to bring themselves as an adult into image as a way of protecting themselves as a child. I also found this technique useful when using the extended focusing task to reprocess painful or traumatic events. Rothschild (2000, 2004) identified that if dissociation occurred whilst a client was attempting to process their trauma material, integration of the new emotional experience and imaginal information is significantly compromised. Therefore, safety must be ensured before any trauma processing can be undertaken.

Babette Rothschild (2001) has a very simple but useful model for processing trauma material, which involves an overarching principal and two phases. The primary aim is to improve the quality of life for the client. The work is not always about trauma repossessing, especially if client doesn't want to. Phase I is about stabilisation and safety. She recommends that you don't move to Phase II before Phase I is achieved. Phase II is the work of processing trauma memories. Once a sense of safety has been established and the client is willing to begin working with their trauma, the trauma-processing work can commence.

I have noticed that if a traumatic memory is accessed within a focusing task via bodily felt sense, in conjunction with emotional arousal and activation of other schematic elements, it is possible to reprocess the event in session in such a way that the person is no longer plagued by the painful aspects of it and is not *retraumatised* by the re-remembering that occurs when asked to retell their story. If the person is able to express the appropriate primary emotion and articulate their needs within the remembered experience, the associated painful emotional charge can be lessened (Elliott, Watson, et al., 2004; Greenberg et al., 1993; Rothschild, 2000). The event is often remembered as having occurred but the emotional intensity is greatly reduced. This reprocessing of the traumatic event is different to a desensitising of that traumatic experience because the client has been able to integrate the experience of the traumatic event without repeated exposure.

In the next section I will describe the research I undertook that helps identify the sequence of the steps for working with a client exhibiting emotional pain.

Research using task analysis

In further research, I used task analysis research methodology to identify the sequence of the proposed expanded focusing task. Task analysis was used by Les Greenberg and Laura Rice in the 1980s to develop EFT, in particular to discover and validate processes of change in clients (Greenberg, 1984a, 1984b, 2007; Rice & Saperia, 1984), so I considered it to be the most appropriate methodology. I was fortunate to have a face-to-face conversation with Robert Elliott who explained to me that the purpose of task analysis is to provide a research methodology that works towards theory-building (R. Elliott, personal communication, 30th June, 2018). The epistemology of dialectical constructivism underpins task analysis. This rational approach to science is neither purely empirical (building models from scratch) nor is it hypothetically deductive (application of an already developed model). The dialectic or dialogue is between the researcher's understanding and the evidence provided by the data. The assumption is that useful understanding will emerge from this interaction. Data is analysed in a systematic and open way. It is important for the researcher not to be attached to the proposed model and to allow the data to inform it as it emerges. In the process of this analysis the model is challenged and improved until it stops changing because of saturation. The resultant empirical model makes sense of the data and provides a model that works (R. Elliott, personal communication, 30th June, 2018).

According to Greenberg (2007), task analysis uses pluralistic methods and engages in intensive observation, model building, measurement construction and testing of hypotheses. It works in the context of both discovery and justification to investigate how people change in psychotherapy. Task analysis evolved out of an *event-based* approach to psychotherapy process research that emphasised the importance of studying process in context (Rice & Greenberg, 1984). An *event* was defined as a clinically meaningful client-therapist interactional sequence that involved a beginning point, a working-through process, and an end point. Greenberg (2007) suggested that task analysis is best done by clinician–scientists who understand the therapeutic process they wish to study, rather than by naive observers or nonclinical researchers.

Greenberg (1984b) explained that task analysis is carried out on one performance by a single individual at one time. A number of cases, all involving the same problem and its resolution, are studied but each analysis is conducted separately. The analysis proceeds in two phases: a discovery-oriented phase and a validation-oriented phase. I conducted research that was discovery oriented and revealed the empirical model, which is seen in Figure 6.1.

In the next section I will present the results from the research I conducted that shows the process of bringing incomplete memories of painful/traumatic events back into awareness in such a way that they can be successfully processed, restructured and integrated.

The final model of the task

Three distinct categories (see Figure 6.1) were identified using the task analysis protocol (Greenberg, 2007). The first category included the marker and the set-up of the task, including grounding, safe place, felt sense symbolisation, and so on. The second category included interaction with episodic memory, dealing with emerging emotions and action tendencies, and reprocessing/rescripting of the memory to resolution. This second category was broken down into event segments. These were points at which the client's state changed and were considered productive. I paid particular attention to the emergence of the primary emotion, and the unmet need and action tendency of the primary emotion, as seen in Table 6.1. Finally, the third category involved the step of carrying forward.

In the second stage of the analysis it was discovered that the way the categories were grouped needed to be revised and renamed as macro-categories. The first of these macro-categories included the marker and the set up of the task and grounding and safe place (see page 87). The second macro-category was reworked to include three substages: Stages 2a, 2b, and 2c. The first sub-stage included creating contact with the felt sense through symbolisation. In this sub-stage, emergence of an episodic memory was fostered. Stage 2b comprised interaction with episodic memory, dealing with emerging emotions, unmet needs and action tendencies, reprocess-

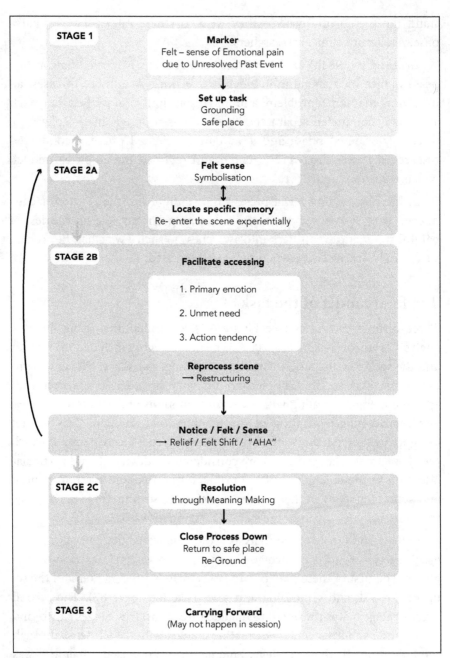

Figure 6.1
Empirical model of extended focusing task as it emerged from the task analysis).

ing/rescripting of memory, and monitoring felt sense. Stage 2 could not be undertaken unless Stage 1 was mastered. The third substage involved the more cognitive process of meaning making, and re-grounding the client back into the here and now. The third macro-category was the carrying forward step. This step includes the client having a deeper understanding of the insights gained by the focusing task, so that they may begin to imagine what their life or situation needs in order for things to be better. The model had undergone a number of refinements until examination of in-session performances yielded no further discoveries (saturation) and a final empirical model was settled upon (Figure 6.1).

What became clear in the second stage of the analysis was the order in which the processing of the unresolved past event occurred. The primary emotion emerged first to uncover the unmet need for that specific event. That in turn led to an action tendency to have that unmet need met. The original concept of the action tendency was that it came out of the primary emotion, but it became clear from the observations of the sessions that the action tendency of the primary emotion needed to happen in conjunction with the accessing of the unmet need. The accessing of the unmet need has its own clear and distinctive role as the transformational element within the task. For example, in the session between John and Betty (described in the Chapter 7) when Betty felt assertive anger, she not only needed to express it but needed to access the unmet need as well in order to stand up for herself with that assertive anger. As she found it difficult to assert herself, her therapist facilitated the act by suggesting she bring in her adult self to do the speaking. Sometimes, accessing the unmet need happens automatically, but the therapist can facilitate this by asking the client: 'What do you need?'. Clients can become stuck at this point because they at the time of the event they felt they were undeserving of having their needs met in that moment. It was also noticed that if the client or therapist tried to meet the unmet need by going to the action tendency too soon before the primary emotion was fully experienced, the client was often unable to say what they needed, or the process did not deepen sufficiently to activate the core primary emotion or emotional pain. In these instances, it was therefore necessary to spend more time to create a more vivid experience of the episodic memory in order to evoke the primary emotion and subsequently find the unmet need.

In addition, when the client entered another aspect of their memory, or another unmet need arose, or an incomplete shift of the felt sense was experienced after the initial reprocessing, the client experientially re-entered their felt sense, re-engaged with that memory or the other emerging memory, and the process was repeated until a full felt shift, full resolution or 'a-ha' was experienced. This is shown by the arrow in Figure 6.1.

For further information on the research behind the development of this extended focusing model see Harte, Strmelj, & Theiler (2019a) and Harte, Strmelj, & Theiler (2019b). At the time of writing, further research is being undertaken to validate the extended focusing task. A smaller outcome study and a detailed examination using the validation phase of task analysis has been given ethics approval.

As a way of illustrating the elements of the extended focusing model, I present in Chapter 7, a research case from my master's research. This single session is a good example of the key components of the task and the unfolding and deepening of the client's experience.

Chapter 7

Working through emotional pain with the expanded focusing task

There are a number of things to consider when working therapeutically with clients who have experienced painful/traumatic events to process these events. The client needs to indicate they are *ready, willing* and *able* to work with the issue/s. As already mentioned, this readiness is identified as a *marker*. The readiness and willingness might be there but are they able? In order to process painful or traumatic events it is essential that the client be equipped to manage it (Rothschild, 2004). Part of this management involves clients being *grounded* in their bodies as dissociation impairs processing.

For many practitioners the experience of a client dissociated in their presence can be very concerning, especially if extreme. In some clients, dissociation is very obvious to witness. But for others we can miss the signs even when the client is sitting in front of us. This is due to many clients having learnt to hide their dissociation or not even being aware they are dissociating. They may have no language for their 'zoning out' or losing a sense of being in the here and now.

Levels of dissociation range on a continuum from its mildest form of daydreaming to the very severe and complex extreme of dissociative identity disorder (DID), where the personality has fragmented as a result of severe trauma. A child looking out of a school window daydreaming or being unresponsive to a parent's requests are classic examples of simple and benign dissociation. Most of us engage in dissociative type behaviours such as driving a car on automatic pilot, watching brainless TV, playing computer games or spending hours on YouTube or Facebook. Most of these endeavours are harmless and actually necessary to manage our stress levels (especially if we are highly sensitive as well; see Chapter 4). It's if these behaviours become chronic and prevent us from connecting with our experiencing selves that this habit of dissociation can be problematic.

For people who have had an accumulation of painful events or severe trauma, dissociation may have been a useful coping or defence mechanism. Being able to dissociate at the time of a traumatic event may have been a very adaptive thing to do. For some people the trauma was so intense — and there was no possibility to flee or fight — that unconscious freezing or dissociating were perceived as the only options for survival. While this may have been adaptive at the time it can become problematic if the person is not able to choose whether they move into a dissociative state or not. When the movement into dissociation is unconscious and not at will, then the client and the therapist need to be able to find strategies and ways to manage this. It's important to mention that it has been strongly suggested that dissociation during a traumatic event predicts the eventual development of posttraumatic stress disorder (PTSD). It has even been suggested that PSTD should be considered a dissociative disorder. The memory goes awry and the person often cannot make sense of their symptoms in the context of the events they have endured. The person is often plagued by state-dependent triggers and/or other classically conditioned associations to their traumas. In simple terms, dissociation is the mind's attempt to flee when flight is not possible, creating a 'split' awareness. Symptoms can involve numbing, flashbacks, depersonalisation, partial or complete amnesia, out-of-body experiences, inability to feel emotion, unexplained irrational behaviours, emotional reactions that seemingly have no basis in reality. Maria and Mick, mentioned in Chapter 2, were clearly showing signs of dissociation.

The limbic system is responsible for all emotional responses. It is the survival centre. It responds to extreme stress by releasing adrenaline and noradrenaline and preparing body for defence and subsequently flight/fight. When flight/fight is not possible, the freeze system is engaged (polyvagal theory). For a person with PTSD, cortisol secretion is not adequate enough to halt the process and so the brain responds as if still under stress/trauma/threat. The cycle persists even though the actual traumatic event has ended, thus creating a chronic state of autonomic nervous system activation: hyperarousal, anxiety, panic, muscle tenseness, concentration problems and sleep disturbances. In some people, reduced hippocampal activity could be a result of the hippocampus never fully developing (attachment deficit), or because it became suppressed (traumatic events), therefore limiting the ability to mediate stress. It may be that for some, later traumatic experiences are remembered only as highly charged emotions and body sensations, whereas for others, the survival mechanism of dissociation or freezing are so habitual that the more adaptive strategies never develop.

Grounding and safe place

When clients are dissociated, not fully in their bodies, this limits access to their experiencing. A simple but effective method for helping clients to be more present in the session is a technique that I developed called *grounding and safe place* (see Table 7.1). I have found that simple mindfulness or meditation techniques are not often practised regularly by my clients, even if they are informed of the benefits. I wanted to develop a process that intuitively made sense and would give immediate benefits. I kept the technique as simple as possible so that my clients would not only remember but might be more likely to engage in the practice. The benefit of this grounding and safe place technique for clients is its simplicity.

My observation is that those people who engage in the grounding and safe place technique to regulate their arousal levels on a very regular basis actually improve more quickly than those who do not. Developing grounding as a new habit counteracts the habit of dissociation and has the potential to change people's quality of life significantly. It has the potential to provide an alternative to anti-anxiety and antidepressant medication. The benefits of using the technique is that it is portable, free of cost, readily

Table 7.1: Grounding and safe place technique

Intention	*Check client is grounded in their body often throughout the trauma processing.* *Particularly important if client is highly aroused or dissociative — highly traumatised clients may find this very difficult.*
STEP 1 **Breath**	Invite client to close eyes (optional) and to become comfortable in their chair. Relax by taking a few deep breaths — notice the in-breath and the outbreath. Emphasise the outbreath to lower arousal. Breathe in for a count of 3 and out for a count of 6 *Breathe out pressure and tension and breathe in calming and relaxing energy.*
STEP 2 **Grounding body**	Slowly invite client to notice: • back against chair • legs on seat of chair • feet on floor • hands in lap etc. *Check by asking if client can get a sense of his/her body sitting in the chair. If not ask him/her to bring awareness to that area and slowly expand to whole body.*
STEP 3 **Safe place**	Encourage client to create an imaginal space or remember a real place where they felt safe, truly relaxed, where no one wanted anything from them. Assists in reducing arousal. Can be alone or with others. Allow time to experience this fully by exploring and describing the scene in detail. Explore with all the senses. *Highly traumatised clients may not have a safe place and therefore not get past this stage. Build up slowly with grounding.* Encourage client to practice regularly and when anxiety or stress increases.

continued over page …

STEP 4 **Anxiety/Stress** **reduction**	Gauge level of anxiety/stress on a scale of 1 to 10 with 10 being very high and 2 to 3 being within normal levels. Ground the client into their body sitting in the chair. Ask them to go to safe place. With each breathe slowly reduce the anxiety/stress until within normal ranges. Breathe out pressure and tension and breathe in calming and relaxing energy
Re-grounding **back into room**	Repeat Step 1 and Step 2 to come back into the room by bringing awareness to breath and body. Then invite client to open their eyes.

available and has no side effects. (Clients should consult their doctor before ceasing any medications.)

The process of grounding and safe place involves three main elements. It is well known that for some, emotion regulation and managing panic attacks can be done by using the breath. However, for many clients with anxiety and trauma, engaging in deep inhalation can actually bring on panic attacks. Bessel van der Kolk (1995) cited research that identified that the outbreath was directly related to the heartbeat and could be used to reduce panic by focusing on a longer exhalation. Encouraging clients to focus more on a longer outbreath rather than a deep 'in breath' made intuitive sense.

The second element involves grounding and using the body as a container. When a person is dissociated, thay are often disconnected from their body. There is a sense of boundarylessness, floating, and at times perceptual distortions. Grounding is achieved by creating body awareness. So, a simple body scan starting by noticing the contact of the back against a chair, noticing the contact of legs on the seat of the chair and feet on the floor offers a sense of body awareness. The aim is to bring awareness to these areas of the body so the whole body can be held in awareness. The direction is also important because moving down the body can aid the mechanism of grounding. Moving up the body may actually activate dissociation. It has also been suggested that meditation is not an appropriate technique for those people who have experienced trauma. I suspect that the 'place' that people 'go to' in meditation may quite likely be where the trauma is stored or compartmentalised. This can leave the person triggered when in fact some sort of relaxation was aimed for. In the past I used the 'clearing the space' technique as suggested by Gendlin but I found many of my clients became dissociated. Therefore, I decided to cease using that part of the focusing model unless the client felt it was useful to help organise thoughts and prioritise a focus for the therapeutic work for that session.

When most people focus on the breath, as suggested in many meditation or mindfulness practices, *unwanted thoughts* tend to intrude. When this happens, one suggestion is to allow the thoughts to pass without attachment to them and bring awareness back to the breath. I found many of my trauma clients had trouble doing this. It's often very difficult for people to silence the mind and to try to combat invasive thoughts with other thoughts of another instruction seemed sometimes impossible for them. Some methods suggest watching the thoughts move as if they are leaves floating down a stream. Using visualisation seemed a better option to me. Imagery has been used in meditative practices and in psychology and psychotherapy from many years. It occurred to me that if we could simultaneously give the mind something to do that also happened to aid a sense of safety then this would add to the ability for a person to ground themselves in their body and support emotional regulation.

The third element is the creation of a *safe place*. I instructed my clients to create a place where they can feel safe. This might be a place that they know quite well or have visited in the past or are willing to create in session. The main elements of the creation of the safe place involve a sense of safety, a feeling of relaxation, a place where 'no one wants anything from them' and a place of peace. This can be very challenging to clients who have experienced trauma as they may have never felt safe in their entire lives. Additionally, some clients cannot visualise so a physiological bodily felt sense of safety can be sufficient. I invite the client to create the safe place as vividly as possible. As this is their imagination they can bring in as many elements of safety as they need. I ask them, 'What do you need to feel safe?', and then suggest, 'Give yourself that'.

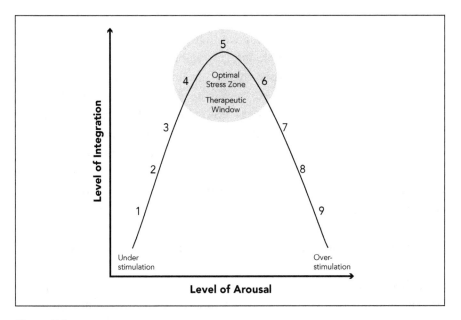

Figure 7.1
The optimal stress zone also coincides with the optimal therapeutic window for integration.

The purpose of grounding and safe place is reducing physiological arousal (Harte, 2012; Rothschild, 2000, 2004). Figure 7.1 indicates the optimal stress zone, which also happens to coincide with the optimal therapeutic window. A way to identify if a client is dissociated is to ask them what their level of anxiety/stress/arousal is on a scale of 1 to 10. I suggest a score of 10 being a high-level arousal and 1 being a low-level arousal. A level of 2 to 3 is considered within normal ranges.

Babette Rothschild (2016) produced a very easy-to-read chart that provides a quick reference to what signs and symptoms we should be looking for in our client. It also assists us to identify if arousal is too high or too low (see www.somatictraumatherapy.com). If we were to map the scores in Figure 7.1 onto the Rothschild chart a level of 2 to 3 would be in the calm (green) area. A score of 4 to 5 would lie in the active/alert (blue) area. Thus, a score of 2 to 5 represents the area for optimal processing and integration of trauma material is very likely to occur at these arousal levels. A low score of 1 would lie in the too low arousal (pale yellow) level and further activation would be needed for effective processing and integration to occur. A score of 6 would indicate that the person is moving into the flight/fight range (orange) where integration becomes less likely. A score of 6 would indicate to the therapist that grounding and safe place techniques need to be implemented immediately so to decrease the levels of arousal prior to any further processing of the trauma material. Scores over 7 should be avoided if possible because the client may fully dissociate and if that occurs the client may lose a sense of where they are and integration is very unlikely to occur. There is no point continuing when dissociation takes the client away from the trauma material they are working with. It is quite remarkable that client sitting in front of you can look calm and yet score of 7 on 10 on the arousal scale. I see it as the responsibility of the therapist to ensure that dissociation does not occur. It indicates to me that the therapist has pushed the client too much into the trauma material and not ensured enough internal safety. It is very important that clients can identify they have entered the early stages of dissociation as well as the therapist remaining empathically attuned in order to identify any signs of dissociation.

Table 7.2: Flashback protocol

Right now, I am feeling _____	Name the emotion here — usually fear
And I am sensing in my body _____	Describe your body sensations — name at least three, if you can.
Because I am remembering _____	Just the name of the trauma or event — no details!
At the same time, I am looking around where I am now in _____	Name the current year, even the month and day
Here, _____	Name where you are right now
And I can see _____	Name things you can see right now, in the room you're in
And so I know _____	Name the trauma again, by title only
Is not happening now/is not happening anymore.	

Source: https://makingsenseoftrauma.com/wp-content/uploads/2016/04/Flashback-Protocol.pdf

If, for some unfortunate reason, a client does dissociate in the session, the flashback protocol developed by Babette Rothschild (2004) is extremely helpful. There are many clients who have experienced severe trauma that are not suitable for processing their painful experiences via the body. The use of the senses can be useful in down-regulating such clients. Asking clients how many things they can see, hear or touch can provide a sense of grounding.

The only homework I ever suggest to clients is to practice the grounding and safe place technique. As I mentioned earlier, those that engage in this practice on a very regular basis and use it to manage their arousal/stress/anxiety levels do much better overall than those that do not. To create the new habit of grounding can require a huge amount of effort for people with anxiety and trauma who rely heavily on dissociation as a means to manage their distress.

Clients may come into the session quite distressed with lots of emotion and teariness. Some therapists think that this emotion is useful to work through. In EFT terms this is regarded as secondary reactive distress and it can have a dissociative quality. Grounding and safe place intervention at the beginning of the session will enable the client to feel more in contact with her body and adaptive emotions are more likely to emerge. The client is more likely to integrate the emerging material as they reprocess their trauma.

Clients need to be confident that their flow of emotion, arousal, memories and body sensations can be contained at will and that they have the ability to move in and out of distressing states. Also, the creation of a safe place before the process began has proven to be useful as it acted as a grounding mechanism or anchor/symbolic location that the client can return to if they become overwhelmed or hyperaroused. For highly trauma-tised clients, developing the grounding and safe place over a period of time assisted them to manage the movement in and out of the painful or trau-matic memories.

Clients who had significant attachment injury are often unable to self-soothe, having never introjected an attentive, caring and soothing caregiver. For many who have experienced trauma for most of their childhood, being externally vigilant was optimal to their survival but resulted in having no opportunity to know or develop their internal experience.

Table 7.3: Steps in processing emotional injury/trauma for a felt sense of emotional pain

Stage 1

Identify marker	Felt sense of emotional pain due to emotional injury/trauma resulting from unresolved past events.
Set up the task	Invite client to participate in task.
Grounding	*Check client is grounded in their body often throughout the process.*
	Particularly important if client is highly aroused or dissociative – highly traumatised clients may find this very difficult.
	Invite client to close eyes (optional) and to become comfortable in their chair.
	Relax by taking a few deep breaths – notice the in-breath and the out-breath.
	Notice back against chair, legs on seat of chair and feet on floor, hands in lap etc.
Safe place	Encourage client to create an imaginal space or remember a real place where they felt safe, truly relaxed, where no one wanted anything from them. Assists in reducing arousal.
	Can be alone or with others.
	Allow time to experience this fully by exploring and describing the scene in detail.
	Highly traumatised clients may not have a safe place and therefore not get past this stage. Build up slowly with grounding.
	Can be used for anxiety/stress reduction.
	Gauge level of anxiety/stress on a scale of 1 to 10 with 10 being very high and 2–3 being within normal levels.
	Ground the client into their body sitting in the chair.
	Ask them to go to safe place.
	With each breath slowly reduce the anxiety/stress until within normal ranges.
	Breath out pressure and tension and breath in calming and relaxing energy.
	Encourage client to practice regularly and when anxiety or stress increases.

Stage 2a

Felt sense	Facilitate development of an internal felt sense.
	Encourage the client to tune into their body sensations.
	Scan body for areas of tension or their unclear feeling.
	Notice where the most pressure and tension is located.

continued over page ...

Stage 2a continued

Symbolic representation	Ask the client to locate and describe the sensation or feeling – it can be a bodily sensation, a symbol, an image, a memory, a hope, a sound, etc.
	Offer exploratory questions to fully search for descriptors e.g. where is it, does it have shape, colour, texture, temperature etc.
	Reflect descriptors back to client – avoiding interpretation.
	Check the accuracy of the symbol/descriptors.
	Ask open-ended questions.
Episodic memory retrieval	Encourage the client to be open to spontaneous awareness.
	Encourage client to focus on bodily felt sense.
	Thoughts or memories may emerge.
	Ask client to be as specific as they can about the memory
	OR
	Ask how long has the bodily felt sensation been there for
	What was going on at that time...?
	Memory emerges.
	Enter the scene experientially.

Stage 2b

Primary emotion	Emotion emerges that can be differentiated.
	The emotion that had been unexpressed may now be expressed.
	A number of primary emotions may be experienced for any given experience.
Access fundamental unmet need	For example, the questions 'what do you need?' and 'what was missing?' can be used and validate the need to be safe, accepted, loved, cared for etc.
Action tendency of primary emotion	• Anger at violation mobilises fight and defence of one's boundaries → *empowerment and assertiveness*.
	• Sadness at loss mobilises reparative grief by either seeking comfort or withdrawal in order to conserve one's resources → *adaptive grieving*.
	• Fear in response to danger mobilises flight, fight or possibly freezing → *adaptive escape*.
	• Disgust organises one to evacuate or withdraw from some noxious experience — *seen in childhood sexual abuse*.

continued over page ...

Stage 2a continued

	• Shame organises one to hide or withdraw from the scrutiny of others — *antidoted by compassion for self.*
	• Surprise or interest — *stimulates curiosity, engagement and facilitates openness to further exploration.*
	• Joy mobilises satisfaction, creativity and happiness — *feels good.*
Reprocess memory	Imaginal restructuring process.
	Bring in the adult/supportive caregiver/to advocate for the child self
	AND/OR
	Remove the child from the traumatic scene – take the child self to the safe place.
Felt shift and Check	Move back and forth from the bodily felt sense or feeling to the thoughts or memories associated with it
	NOTICE *FELT SHIFT*: Felt shifts deepen understanding because of the consonance between the felt experience, emerging symbols and emerging meaning.
	Clients may get a sense of relief, describe an 'a-ha' moment, a deeper understanding.
	If felt sense not shifted or experience not fully processed return to Step 2a and repeat process.

Stage 2c

Meaning	Resolution through meaning making.
	Encourage client to stay with new or emerging experience and understating.
	May or may not happen in the session.
Return to safe place and Re-Grounding	Invite client to return to safe place.
	Bring client back to their awareness of their body in the chair in the room.
	Invite client to notice their breath – notice the in-breath and the out-breath.
	To become aware of their body in the chair – their back against chair, legs on seat of chair and feet on floor, hands in lap etc.

---

continued over page ...

Stage 3

Carrying forward action tendency	Having a deeper understanding of the insights gained by the focusing, the client may begin to imagine what in their life or situation needs to be changed.
	This may take the client further into exploration, offer insight into action strategies or provide a sense of achievement and completeness.
Full resolution	May occur in session or out of session.

Source: Harte (2017).

The case of Betty

As a way of illustrating the elements of the expanded focusing model, I present a case from my master's research. The process steps are described in Table 7.3. This single session is a good example of the key components of the task and the unfolding and deepening of the client's experience.

Betty had a history of 'small t' trauma. Her father, while basically a good man, had significant issues with over-controlling behaviour, anger and aggression. While not violent, her father was demanding of Betty's compliance in a way that made her fearful. The session began with Betty feeling really overwhelmed and shaky with a strong felt-sense in her chest. She wasn't sure what it was about. She was teary. She had fragmented images of her father floating around the edge of her awareness but nothing stood out as distinctive. John, her therapist, saw her distress and suggested she ground herself. He did this by inviting her to close her eyes, evoke body awareness and create a safe space (Stage 1). This intervention served the purpose of reducing the level of Betty's arousal to assist John in identifying whether the arousal was part of an appropriate emotional response or an undifferentiated distress response such as dissociation. John used a simple scale to assess Betty's level of anxiety. A higher score indicated a high level of arousal or possible dissociation. She stated that her anxiety was 7/10. A level of 2 to 3 is considered within the normal range. This higher level of arousal could hinder productive processing and later integration (Rothschild, 2011). Stage 1 aimed to foster optimal emotional internal experiencing and was done by grounding the client, connecting her into her body, creating safety, establishing emotional distance from the pain and fostering emotion regulation. (Stage 2 should not be undertaken unless Stage 1 is mastered).

Once Betty had reached a lower state of arousal (4/10), John was able to invite Betty to bring her attention to her felt sense. She explained she had tension in her throat and upper chest (Stage 2a). Betty was experiencing emotional distress or secondary reactive sadness. As she was acutely present to her emotional pain searching for it to emerge from her felt sense was not necessary. John invited her to stay with the experience but as the intensity increased she again became dissociative. John attended to her dissociation by re-grounding her back into her body and assisted her to distance herself/establish a safe distance from the experience by explaining to her what might be happening. This helped Betty to refocus. She noticed that she was tapping her foot (a felt-sense). She described a feeling of frustration as more memories of her father emerged. This seemed to be about something that he did that she was not happy with. He had frightened her. John invited Betty to bring to mind an image of her father. What arose next was an episodic memory. She recalled an event when she was 15 years old, when she had managed to obtain an interview for a part-time job (Stage 2a). Her father tried to stop her attending the interview by yelling at her and forbidding her to go. Her mother, however, supported her going to the interview and they headed towards the car to leave. As they got into the car her father went to the garage and got a pickaxe. While he did not use the axe as a weapon he kicked the car on her mother's side and yelled at them to stop as her mother started to move the car out of the driveway. As Betty described the event she got in touch with her primary fear and her arousal levels again escalated (Stage 2b.1). John asked Betty what 'younger Betty' needed in that moment to feel safe (Stage 2b.2). Betty said that younger Betty needed to get out of the driveway because she felt stuck in the car (Stage 2b.3). She said the car was not leaving and John suggested she use her mind to take her adult self and her 15-year-old self to her safe place (Stage 2b, reprocessing the scene). The action tendency, while not directly related to the scene, created an exit opportunity (adaptive escape) that had not been available at the real time of this event. Following action tendency activated a sense of relief in Betty that reduced her distress and arousal levels significantly. Her breathing returned to normal levels and she became calm. Betty was able to imagine her adult and younger self in their safe place, being on a beach, sitting on the sand looking at the water. John checked in with how Betty was feeling, and she stated that she was okay.

John invited Betty to go back into the experience to see if she could reprocess it further or access other memories. She was able to recall other events at 14 or 15 when her father had not heard her and had stopped her from doing things she wanted to do. This activated primary shame. Her head lowered as she cowered at recalling the memories. John asked Betty to bring her father into the scene and ensured that safety measures were in place before doing this. Betty was able to put her father 'in a bubble' so he couldn't talk back to her but could hear her and acknowledge that he heard her. Betty's adult self was able to speak on behalf of her younger self about what it was like for her to not be heard. She accessed primary assertive anger, the antidote to primary maladaptive shame (Stage 2b.1). John encouraged her to ask for what she needed as clearly as she could (Stage 2b.2) and she asserted that she needed him to see her and support her to be 'who I am … and not make me something different' (Stage 2b.3). She repeated a number of times 'let me be who I am', supported by John, who repeated the phrase with her. As she did this repeatedly, Betty's body posture changed and shifted, and she sat upright in her chair. She described feeling relief in her chest (felt shift). John checked to see if there was anything else she wanted to say to her father before they asked him to leave. Some preliminary meaning-making emerged at this point. Betty said that her father's influence had impacted her decisions in her career path and she was angry about that.

John encouraged Betty to go back to her safe place as she watched her father's bubble float off into distance. She decided to leave her words with her father, realising she could come back to this later if she needed to. John re-grounded Betty back into the present moment (Stage 2c). Further meaning making emerged as Betty also became aware of how she always had to be somebody else and not herself. She said, 'Now it is okay for me to be me.' Betty explained that this was a big realisation for her but she was not quite sure how this might change things for her in the future (Stage 3). The action of carrying forward the newly understood information does not always happen within the session.

As described in Chapter 3, there is a specific adaptive action tendency for each primary emotion. In Betty's successful session, she was able to access her primary emotion, get her unmet need met, and imaginally take action. She could access primary adaptive anger and express it by standing up for what her child self was entitled to. Accessing primary adaptive anger has been suggested to be at the core of the transformation of emotional pain (see Greenberg, 2011; Timulak, 2015). The action tendency of standing up for the child self allowed Betty to recover agency and control, which in turn energised her to ask for her unmet needs to be met. The ensuing sense of entitlement was affirming and provided her with a sense of personal power that counterbalanced the fear and hopelessness that is often present in emotional pain (Timulak, 2015). This action was accompanied by a felt shift. The ability to access adaptive anger can vary amongst clients. Some are more able to access their adaptive anger easily whilst others do so more tentatively. Betty's therapist's ability to normalise and encourage healthy anger expression was important, as expression of anger in any form may not be acceptable to many clients. Betty also experienced primary fear and she was supported and facilitated by her therapist to create safety for her younger self in the face of this by allowing her adult self to provide protection or to exit the scene.

Betty's session is an illustration of how a number of primary emotions may emerge in a process. It was evident that if one unmet need became processed then another unprocessed unmet need arose. Once Betty's primary fear was worked through and she felt safe and protected her primary adaptive anger emerged. This was the anger that she needed to express at the age of 15 but was unable to. This primary adaptive anger could be seen as an antidote to the previously felt fear. Assertive anger provided a sense of entitlement to be loved, acknowledged and secure. The expression of adaptive anger is at the core of the transformation of emotional pain (Greenberg, 2011; Timulak, 2015). In my opinion, the car was still not fully integrated, as Betty was not able to re-enter that scene and imagine being assertively angry with her father. The memory that emerged was a less emotionally provocative scene that she could potentially process more comfortably. Further sessions may see Betty work through these and other events until she no longer holds emotional pain or psychological distress about her father's behaviours. Thus, '[t]he past can be changed, at least the memories of it' (Greenberg, 2015, p. 10).

Follow up with Betty

Betty was asked to provide a follow-up comment about her single session with John. It is presented verbatim:

> Since that session, I think over two years ago now, I have repositioned my relationship with my father in a felt way. While he still disrespects me verbally on occasion, I am much less disturbed and hurt by his negativity. I feel unstuck, and I've been able to move forward with a sense of myself that was shut down, in part by him, many years ago.
>
> I have returned to the pleasure of making art, which I did as a child and teenager with some success. My father stopped me from pursuing an artists' life. But I have returned to my creative work, despite his recent declaration, 'you're not an artist', and am currently participating in my fifth exhibition. I feel that I can protect myself sufficiently from his barbs and explore just being me. I'm not stuck, I can assert myself and create my own safety in his presence.
>
> I don't become as anxious as I used to when I know we will see each other. I imagine him often in his bubble, frail, deformed, small and afraid himself. This image evokes compassion for him and his own fears and limitations, but they no longer hold me. I don't need him to see me so much anymore, I'm not sure he really can. He did attend one exhibition last year and was clearly uncomfortable, but he did try to engage with my work. At least on that occasion he didn't feel it necessary to turn my work upside down in order for it to make sense to him.
>
> When I try to remember that scene now, I struggle, it's just not very clear and doesn't have the intensity of feeling attached to it. I know I got out of there and I can continue to get myself out of a fearful space with him, I'm not helpless. He doesn't really scare me so much anymore, even though he can still threaten to be violent.
>
> One of the most important parts of the session I think was being able to be angry with him for his stupid behaviour, that has given me energy to protect myself and not accept that it was okay. The other thing is the image I have of him in the bubble. That keeps me calm and compassionate around him. Because I do love him very much. Overall, I feel like the session made me feel strong, that I can manage what's happened, and be me and be okay.

As explained at the end of Chapter 6, I implemented task analysis that enabled me to build a model of a task that illustrated how therapeutic change occurred for clients who presented with a felt sense of emotional pain due to an unresolved painful/traumatic event. A three-stage *empirical model* emerged from the analysis. This empirically derived model describes a task for *processing emotional injury or trauma* when the marker is identified as a *felt sense of emotional pain*.

The case of John and Betty illustrated the sequence of the task. A strong working alliance provided a safe therapeutic environment for the client to be facilitated along the revealed pathway to resolution. Stage 1 aimed to foster an optimal internal *experiencing* by creating a focusing space and to develop contact with a client's internal world. This was done by grounding the client in her body, creating a sense of external and internal safety, establishing emotional distance, and fostering emotional regulation. It was vital that the client was able to enter, process, and leave her inner experience at will before moving to Stage 2. The second stage involved the therapist facilitating access to a specific episodic memory via the body through their felt sense. The aim here was to bring to awareness a memory associated with the emotional pain that might be incomplete or out of awareness but activated in the present moment through the felt sense. This process opened up awareness of early childhood needs that had not been met and which could now be addressed. Once that unmet need for that experience had been accessed, the action tendency of the primary emotion motivated the client to find agency. For example, Betty in her imagination was be able to stand up for her child self with assertive anger, thus activating the entitlement to be seen as an individual by her father. The imagery, together with activation of the primary emotion, the accessing of the unmet need and the client taking some sort of action that emerged from that primary emotion created a shift or resolution. The episodic memory was potentially no longer a symbol of that unmet need and Betty could leave it, or let it go. The primary emotion had been discharged and the resolution was signified by a felt shift or an 'a-ha' moment.

A number of key elements are important when undertaking the expanded focusing task. These are developing a solid therapeutic alliance; keeping arousal levels within the window of tolerance levels that allow for integration of the newly accessed material and avoid dissociation; allowing the body to bring an episodic memory to awareness through facilitation of the felt sense; staying with *experience*; activating the primary emotion; identifying the unmet need; and promoting the action tendency of the primary emotion.

Betty's experiencing style was one of being able to remain present to feelings and internal processes. She was able to link and integrate new information as it occurred in the present. Her arousal level was identified as very intense as she freely expressed her emotion with voice and body, and there was spontaneous expression of emotion with almost no sense of restriction. Her emotional productivity indicated that the emotion that was experienced, was expressed and led to resolution such as a sense of relief, 'aha' moment or felt shift.

The working alliance for John and Betty was measured as strong. It is clearly documented that the working alliance is an important change factor (see Norcross, 2010, for a review). This is consistent with other research on humanistic psychotherapies showing that the alliance is an essential ingredient in the process of change (Elliott, Greenberg, & Leitaer, 2004). EFT emphasises the importance of the working alliance and thus provides a good framework for developing a good alliance (Elliott, Watson, et al., 2004; Greenberg et al., 1993). Although the session with John and Betty does not prove that a good working alliance is *required* in order for the expanded focusing task to work, it does appear likely given that people may not be able to approach strong emotions without the feeling of interpersonal safety that is implicit in a strong working alliance.

The concept of *staying with the experience* is relevant when discussing the elements of successful processing. Adaptive primary emotions by their very nature tend to arise and dissipate quickly. With a natural rising and falling in intensity, they feel right for the given situation and have adaptive qualities (Elliott, Watson, et al., 2004). Clients need to be able to master Stage 1 which allows them to move through the discomfort and distress of their maladaptive secondary and primary emotions to uncover the primary emotion that is connected with their unmet need. They need to be able to move to an adaptive action tendency necessary for successful processing of their painful/traumatic events. It appears *staying with* experience is central to this.

The strength of this model is that it tracks experience and not just emotion. While Gendlin's Focusing task encouraged people to stay with and talk from their current experience (Gendlin, 1981, 1996), Greenberg asked clients to talk from their presently felt emotion (Greenberg, 2011). This expanded Focusing or Trauma Processing task asks the client to speak intentionally from their emotional and experiential child self and encourages them to express their unmet need/s, thus capturing both the processing of their experience and their emotion simultaneously.

The session with John and Betty revealed that when there was a reactivation of a long-term memory there was a possibility of updating that memory. Betty reported in the follow-up discussion that the memory had a different quality to it. It was more difficult to remember as it wasn't very clear and didn't have the same emotional intensity as prior to the session. She felt less attached to it. She reported that she had 'got out' and didn't feel trapped or 'helpless'. This supports the findings of Hupbach et al. (2007) and Lane et al. (2015) that by accessing the primary emotion and providing new input that activated an action tendency to facilitate the meeting of an unmet need into the original memory, a situation was created where there was a hypothetical disconnection of the unexpressed emotion from the original memory. This in turn may provide an alternative neural pathway that, if reinforced through many such processing sessions, will assist in breaking down the neural patterning that led to the psychological symptoms of emotional pain. Accessing a primary emotion through memory retrieval and providing new input can activate an action tendency to facilitate the meeting of an unmet need for the client. Therefore, hypothetically, there is a disconnection of the unexpressed primary emotion from the original memory. Betty was able to express primary adaptive fear and primary adaptive anger. This process could be considered more than desensitisation or rescripting as it has the potential to be transformational and restructuring. Betty was able to feel safe enough and empowered enough to actualise alternative scenarios that facilitated a sense of resolution. She reported that the session was helpful in assisting her to understand the connections between past unresolved events and the present and provided a sense of relief. She no longer feels impacted by her father's criticism and has returned to creative pursuits that were once criticised by her father. So it appears, as Betty described in her follow up statement that the episodic memory is no longer a symbol of her unmet needs, nor does it activate her emotional pain around this episode.

John and Betty's session supports existing theoretical frameworks that attempt to explain how important it is to access primary emotions because they are biologically adaptive responses that reflect survival needs (Elliott, Watson, et al., 2004; Greenberg & Safran, 1987, 1989; Izard, 1977; Paivio &

Pascual-Leone, 2010; Timulak, 2015). Primary emotions are clearly linked to action tendencies in a way that reflect these earlier findings and theory. For example, fear was related to an action tendency around self-protection, and anger was related to an action tendency around asserting the self. Pascual-Leone and Greenberg (2007) explained that 'assertive anger is essentially anger that has enough differentiation to embody a positive self-evaluation and the clear assertion of that evaluation or of some personal need' (p. 879). Assertive anger is about setting boundaries and engaging in a fight for one's rights and/or existential needs. These findings can directly relate to psychotherapy practice by helping therapists to better understand how to make sense of and work with emotions in their clients.

Betty was able to access her bodily felt sense and stay with her experience, which provided a pathway to accessing and working with her traumatic memories. This is consistent with modern somatic psychotherapies (Levine, 2015; Ogden, 2006; Ogden & Fisher, 2015), and their contention that trauma can best be conceptualised and worked with at the level of bodily exploration (Rothschild, 2000). Betty was able to stay with intense but not overwhelming levels of emotional arousal. Emotional experiencing in session needs to be sufficient without being overwhelming (Greenberg, 2011; Lane et al., 2015; Rothschild, 2011); that is, a zone of optimal arousal. For example, as seen in Table 7.1, the task has built into it ways in which a therapist can help a client move forward (by focusing on the felt sense) and away (by grounding and *safe place* visualisation) from overwhelming inner experience as seen in the session with Betty.

There is a relationship between the expanded focusing for a felt sense of emotional pain and unfinished business using an empty chair task as discussed by Elliott, Watson, et al., (2004). It has been shown that using an empty-chair technique to confront an inadequate or abusive parent or significant other can be extremely effective in resolving emotional injuries (Elliott, Watson et al., 2004; Paivio & Pascual-Leone, 2010). The expanded focusing task uses a similar technique but within the imagination to effectively manage the confrontation without having to use chairs. Some clients struggle to embrace the chair technique because it may seem too confrontational and potentially overwhelming (Paivio & Pascual-Leone, 2010). Paivio found that what she described as 'imaginal confrontation' was a good alternative to the empty-chair work (Paivio & Pascual-Leone, 2010). In this task she asked clients to maintain eye contact with the therapist rather than engage in a dialogue with an imagined other. The client is encouraged to express their thoughts and feelings to the therapist rather than with the imagined other. According to Paivio and Pascual-Leone (2010) research supports the view that this procedure is less stressful than using an empty chair. The expanded Focusing task emphasises safety for the client and so offers an alternative to the empty-chair technique popularised in EFT.

Essentially this model introduces an EFT frame to focusing. The felt sense as described by Gendlin (1981, 1996) is used in a different way and for a different purpose. This model uses the felt sense to activate the emotional pain related to unmet needs that were unable to be met. In order to work with this emotional pain, the client needs to feel safe enough to do so. EFT emphasises the interpersonal safety that is provided by the therapist. This model emphasises the idea that intrapsychic safety can be developed through grounding and use of an imagined safe place. The client learns through the therapist's direction, how to create their own safety and to develop their own relationship to their own experience that then allows them to process their trauma or difficult maladaptive early childhood experiences that they hadn't been able to do in the past.

Chapter 8

Chair work and emotional pain

Emotion focused therapy (EFT) is strongly identified as using chair work as one of its main interventions, and a long research history using the chair tasks. For example, Greenberg published a very early paper in 1979, entitled Resolving Splits: The Two-Chair Technique. However, for many clients, the idea of engaging in chair work and moving from one chair to another is a daunting task. A client with a significant trauma history may have fragmented or fragile sense of self. Thus, it might be prudent to suggest that unless the client's sense of self is sufficiently robust it may not be appropriate to engage in chair work initially. In my work with trauma clients, I found it more useful to use the extended focusing task in the earlier stages of therapy because it appeared to assist in strengthening the client's sense of self. However, the chair work is particularly effective for working with intrapsychic conflict that results from the introjected voice or voices of significant others and can be more useful in the later stages of therapy.

Dialectical constructivism

The developers of EFT proposed a *dialectical constructivist* view of human functioning to explain how people make sense of their emotions (Greenberg, 2004; Greenberg & Pascual-Leone, 1995, 2001; Greenberg & Watson, 2006). Dialectical constructivism is the epistemology on which EFT is based, with 'dialectical' defined as the art of discussion or debate. Dialectics, in its most essential form, is the splitting of a single whole into its contradictory parts. From the perspective of *dialectical constructivism*, the *self* is a constantly changing but organised multiplicity (Elliott, Watson, Goldman, & Greenberg, 2004), seen as a dynamic self-organising system that is influenced by interaction with the environment moment by moment (Greenberg, 2011).

In dialectical constructivist terms, the self is a multi-process, multi-level organisation emerging from the dialectical interaction of many component elements (Greenberg & Pascual-Leone, 1995, 2001). Internal and external reality is viewed fundamentally as a process of constructing views of self and world from constituents that actually exist as constraints on one's constructions. The self is a viewed as a process and not a structure. People are complex, dynamic, self-organising systems, organised collections of various multiple aspects. There is no permanent, nor such thing as a true self but more like a chorus of 'voices' or singers performing a complicated piece of modern music or jazz. These difference aspects or voices often form conflicting parts that define and oppose each other.

What is identified in dialectical constructivist terms is *true self experience*. These are moments where there is no internal conflict, often described as 'a-ha' moments of experience. It might transpire through a deep and meaningful emotional experience that makes things significant and can occur when accessing core emotions or during moments of deep connection with others. What is being experienced is real, deep and true, and signifies an experience of one's *true self*.

Stability is experienced when people regularly recreate themselves out of the same basic component elements as they interact with their situation (Elliott, Watson, et al., 2004). Such stability arises from repeated constructions of the same state from multiple, constituent elements that are constructed, afresh, each time. These characteristic organisations impart character to the person, and are responsible for the more enduring aspects of personality. Adding or subtracting elements from the process of construction can alter these traits, making *character change* possible (Greenberg & Pascual-Leone, 1995, 2001). Dialectical synthesis of emotion and reflection is the key to therapeutic change (Greenberg & Pascual-Leone, 1995, 2001).

Dialectical constructivism has several implications for understanding how people change in therapy (Elliott, Watson, et al., 2004). Much of the therapeutic work for the client involves various internal dialectical processes where separation and contact between different aspects are facilitated (Elliott & Greenberg, 1997). Evocation and explication of the various implicit self aspects and facilitation of psychological contact with those aspects results in a new integrative experience of self. Previously overlooked or silenced voices are encouraged to emerge so that the more dominant voices can hear those hitherto ignored voices and an internal self-challenge is created (Elliott, Watson, et al., 2004). Assimilation and accommodation occur with both aspects undergoing change. Dialectical processes can be observed in the conceptualising versus experiencing domains of the client, and in the 'splits' between the dominant voice that reiterates negative views of self, versus a less dominant, more change-orientated voice of life and growth (Elliott, Watson, et al., 2004).

There are two major sources of experience: a conscious, controlled, deliberate, serial, reflexive conceptual process (thinking); and an automatic, direct, parallel processing of information, schematic emotional process (feeling) occurring out of awareness. There is a constructive, dialectical relationship between the two sources of experience. Clients make sense of their experience by symbolising their bodily felt sensations into awareness and articulating them into language, thereby constructing new meaning. Therapists assist clients to change their experiencing by helping them attend to different aspects of self. Such a dialectical process requires both separation and contact between both sides. The enactment tasks in EFT, particularly the two-chair work, are a means in which to work with these dialectical processes.

There are three types of chair work. The first task is two-chair dialogue for conflict splits and the second task is a two-chair enactment for interruptive processes. The third is empty-chair work for unfinished business with significant others. We will now look at these in turn.

Two-chair dialogue for conflict splits

Many difficulties that people experience are the result of a conflict between an image of themselves and what Carl Rogers referred to as their self-actualising tendency or in EFT terms, their experiencing self. People operate according to their 'shoulds' rather than paying attention to their feelings and needs. A healthy organism 'knows' what is good for it and will thus integrate the good and reject what is not (Perls, Hefferline, & Goodman, 1951). The self is seen to consist of different parts and to function adequately involves integrating polarities. Otherwise, people are troubled by cognitive dissonance that manifests in two opposing sides: 'I should do this, but I can't'. 'Part of me wants this, but another part of me wants that'. 'I want to leave, but I want to stay' 'I want to do this, but I am inadequate'. Similarly, they can be tormented by negative self-evaluations: 'I'm a failure'. 'I'm worthless'. 'I'm a bad person'.

The marker for the two-chair dialogue is self-criticism or feelings of being torn. Two aspects of self are opposing each other. In Australia, the EFT community have modified the two-chair dialogue and actually work with four chairs (see Figure 8.1). The therapist moves with the client to provide support and encourage the client to stay on task. This has been reported by many clients as extremely reassuring, particularly when their inner critic is harsh. Having said this, the classic chair work described by Greenberg is extremely effective as the research shows. Also, some therapists may not have enough room to put four chairs in their consulting rooms.

The therapist encourages the client to collaborate in the task. For many clients it feels very awkward to be talking to different aspects of themselves represented in chairs, so it is recommended to suggest that the client sees this as a *role-play* until they feel more engaged. The chairs are set up as in Figure 8.1. It is really important to identify which is the critical voice in opposition to the experiencing self. Stage 1 involves setting up the task with a clear identification of the critical voice to ensure a successful outcome. In order to deepen the split it is important to encourage the critic to be quite harsh (being careful not to let it be too blaming, overbearing and destructive) and very specific in its delivery of criticism. This enables the experiencing self to differentiate their emotional response, which in turn helps to clarify and focus the process. The therapist invites the client to speak as the critic to the other chair. This activates the experiencing self in such a way that the client may find their voice.

In Stage 2, the client is invited to swap chairs and the therapist asks them what it felt like to be on the receiving end of the harsh criticism. It is suggested to the client to notice their bodily felt sense as a way of deepening the process. Often the critic is an introjected voice of a parent or a significant other. It is then useful to ask the client to identify who this voice or criticism reminds the client of and then engage in empty-chair work as described in the section below. An interaction between the experiencing self and the introjected other takes place. The experiencing self may remember some childhood issue where the parent or significant other was unavailable physically, psychologically, emotionally and unable to meet the client's needs. If a significant other is not identified, Stage 3 is enacted.

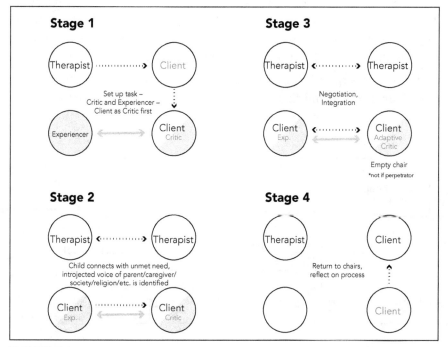

FIGURE 8.1

The use of four chairs for resolving a conflict split

In Stage 3, the client's unfinished business with the client's parent or significant other has reached a conclusion and the therapist asks them to invite the parent or significant other to leave that chair. An interaction between what now appears to be a softened critic, known as the adaptive critic, and experiencing self is facilitated by the therapist. Is important to enable expression from both sides. The therapist facilitates a negotiation between adaptive critic and experiencing self in relation to practical compromises. Ultimately, compassion emerges from the adaptive critic towards the experiencing self that leads to self-acceptance. The adaptive critic actually has a protective quality. Its role is to ensure the experiencing self remains safe, like a well-functioning parent would. It often holds the morals and values within the individual. Unfortunately, because of the introjected critical parent or significant other, the voice can become berating and undermining. The client may be quite confused at this point as to which chair is which. This is actually a sign of integration. Stage 4 sees the client and the therapist return to their original chairs. This actually helps the client to be able to reflect on the process and energetically leave it, and it is particularly important when only partial resolution has been possible. It allows the client to get some distance and creates more safety.

Les Greenberg (1984a) used task analysis to identify the steps in the two-chair dialogue and this is illustrated in Figure 8.2. The first box indi-

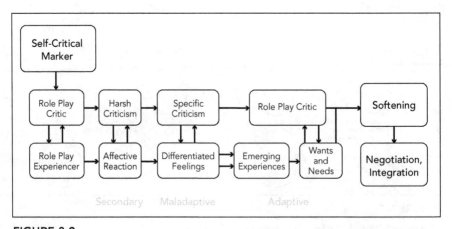

FIGURE 8.2

Steps in empty-chair work for conflict split Source: Greenberg, et al (1993)

cates the marker of self-criticism, and the first set of boxes indicate the processes occurring in the chair of the critic. The second row of boxes are the processes that occur for the experiencing self. See *Learning Emotion-Focused Therapy* for more detailed accounts of the chair work (Elliott, Watson, et al., 2004).

At times, the experiencing self may collapse under the belief that their critic is right, and thus the critic possesses the only dominant voice. This is what we call in EFT an interruptive process. Resignation is an interruptive process, and the resultant state is a sense of shame, helplessness, powerlessness, and hopelessness. Validation of these states helps to activate primary anger and sadness that need expression. A variety of interruptive mechanisms, such as interjections and projections, block awareness and prevent contact with the environment and need satisfaction. Other phenomena, such as conflict between polarities, unfinished business, habits, avoidance and catastrophising also block awareness and the satisfaction of needs, and produce dysfunction. The therapist must be alert to recognise self-interruptions in the client, because the progress and energy of the session can go quite flat when an interruptive process is present. The person may describe or begin to express a feeling, need or action but somehow blocks the expression. This restriction or interruption of feeling, need or action might be described by the client or observed by the therapist. The client expresses distress or discontent as a result of the interruption that may include physical pain. Internally, the inner experience that goes with the self-interruption is a feeling of being 'blocked' or 'stopped'. Figure 8.3 illustrates this process.

Interruptive processes were actually formed at key developmental stages in the client's life. They are generally responses to environments that did not allow for full expression of emotions and needs. Often, they are learned responses designed to cope with an unsafe environment or may be an internalised lack of entitlement. These behaviours continue as automatic reactions that prevent full expression of emotion and experience. The interruptive processes were adaptive at the time, but not anymore.

Essentially, the marker for the self-interruptive split task is for blocked feelings and resignation, where one part interrupts another part. Self-interruption is more likely to be experienced within another task rather than in being set up as a task on its own. For example, if the client becomes blocked

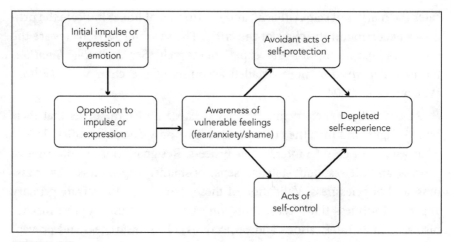

FIGURE 8.3

Interruptive processes.

whilst engaging in a conflict split task, some time and attention may be needed to assist the client to move past the self-interruptive block.

If the client has a predominant style of self-interruption, it might be useful to set up a task as a discrete task on its own. The therapist will set up the chairs as in Figure 8.1 but instead of the critic sitting in the critic chair, the self-interrupter takes its place. The therapist encourages the client to actively enact self-interruptive processes in a very concrete and specific manner by asking the client *how* they interrupt themselves. The client swaps chairs and responds to the interrupter. The therapist invites the client to notice their bodily felt sense and to express what it is like to be on the receiving end of the interruption. This way it is possible to identify or differentiate the self-interrupter and the interrupted expression. As in the conflict split it is very likely the interrupter is an internalised or introjected voice of a significant other, usually a parent. The therapist invites the experiencing self to fully express themselves and to stimulate and support emerging assertiveness. The end goal is about freedom of self-expression and empowerment. Figure 8.4 illustrates the steps involved in the self-interruptive split. See *Learning Emotion-Focused Therapy* for more detailed accounts of the chair work (Elliott, Watson, et al., 2004).

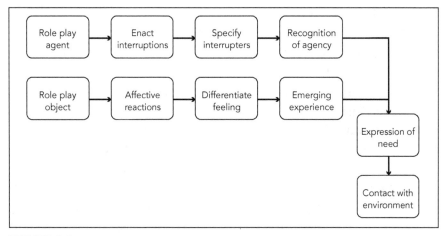

FIGURE 8.4

Steps in empty-chair work for interruptive processes. Source: Greenberg, et al (1993)

Empty-chair for unfinished business with significant others

The empty-chair technique is based on the Gestalt principle that significant unmet needs do not fully recede from awareness. Fritz Perls, founder of Gestalt therapy, and Jacob L. Moreno, founder of psychodrama, explain the empty-chair technique differently. Perls et al. (1951) believed the client should imagine an absent person in an empty chair. Moreno (1946) believed the client should reverse roles and become the absent person. Therein lies the fundamental difference between Gestalt therapy and psychodrama and the use of the empty-chair technique. From an EFT perspective, when specific emotion schemes associated with significant others are triggered, the person re-experiences unresolved emotional reactions. The unfinished quality of that relationship will continue to intrude, often unconsciously, on current relationships.

There are two types of empty-chair enactments: One for neglect or abandonment, and the other for abuse or trauma. In both, the representation of the other in the chair serves a function that is integral to the resolution of the dialogue. Neglect or abandonment can be by significant others (e.g., parents and caregivers), but also from current relationships, those who have passed away, or are otherwise no longer physically available. This can also be a useful task in supervision where a client has suddenly terminated therapy without explanation. The supervisee may be confused as to what actually happened in the last session and unpacking the experience in such a way can help clarify the situation somewhat.

In the case of trauma or neglect the perpetrator could be a friend, lover, or caregiver. The trauma could be single incident or repeated victimisations over several years. This task is contraindicated when there is a risk of retraumatisation, suicidality or aggressive behaviour. Because the empty chair can be a highly evocative technique with increased arousal, assisting the client to ground is very important (see Chapter 6). A client can be quite dissociated without the therapist realising and so checking in with the client is very important. The advanced attunement fosters close tracking by the therapist and ensures safety. Integration cannot occur if the client is dissociated. A useful method to ensure safety for the client is to be flexible as to where the empty chair is placed. If it is too close, suggest moving it away. If the room is not large enough, imagine a glass shield in front of the parent or significant other. It might even be appropriate to imagine the other in the dock of a courtroom surrounded by guards. The main thing is to ensure that the arousal in the client is not too high as the process would be retraumatising and ineffective in resolving the unfinished business. Encourage the client to do grounding if arousal does become too high as described in Chapter 6.

Once the marker for unfinished business is identified the therapist invites the client to engage in the task, and sets up that task with four chairs for Stage 1 as illustrated in Figure 8.5. One of the key factors is to help the client make psychological contact with, or evoke the presence of the other. This may not be a full image but even a sense of the person will suffice. This is done by asking the client to imagine what the age is of the parent or significant other, what they are wearing, and noting what the expression is on the client's face as they reply. This is a characteristic of EFT where the therapist invites the client to notice what is going on internally and explain that in felt sense terms. The therapist uses empathetic explorative responses and encourages the client to use first-person language. The client begins by blaming, complaining or expressing hurt or longing in relation to a significant other. The client speaks to the imagined other and expresses unresolved feelings of resentment or hurt. It is important for the therapist to recognise and distinguish primary emotion and secondary emotions in the client. Primary mal-

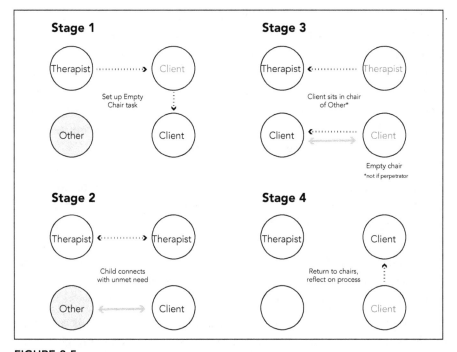

FIGURE 8.5

The use of four chairs in empty-chair enactment for unfinished business with a significant other.

adaptive emotions will have a stuck quality and sound repetitive. Secondary reactive emotions have a defensive quality and there is a sense there is something deeper underneath. If the client differentiates their original complaint into an emotional response such as their primary adaptive emotion and experiences and expresses that relevant emotion with a comfortable degree of arousal there is likely to be a shift in awareness and understanding.

The main emphasis here is for the client to identify what were their unmet needs and what was the impact of not having those unmet needs met (Stage 2). The unmet needs have to be validated, as every child deserves to be loved, protected and seen. The therapist helps the client explore and express those unmet needs more assertively and provide empathic affirmation for the emotion that is often present as the unmet needs emerge.

Ultimately, as the client engages in the dialogue with the significant other it becomes evident that it is unlikely that the parent or significant other is able to meet the needs of the client. This often can be extremely painful for the client and they may not be able to let go of the idea that their parents should meet their needs. It may take a number of empty chair enactments for this to become fully realised. An important part of the process is for the therapist to encourage the client to see the other in new ways, perhaps in a more positive light or the other as a less powerful person who has problems of their own. But it is important where there has been traumatic abuse perpetrated by a significant other that the client does not spend too much time being compassionate to the other or considering the other's position. Children who have been traumatised often spend a great deal of time over-identifying with their perpetrating parent, or making excuses for them, such as, 'They had a hard life and they did the best they could'. This is a survival technique but also interrupts or minimises the client's true response to the abuse they have endured or are enduring. The goals of the task are letting go of resentments and unmet needs in relation to the other, as well as self-affirmation, understanding or holding the other accountable.

A potential important, yet challenging variation of the task is to ask the client to sit in the chair of the other (Stage 3). If it is safe enough for the client to do so it can be very illuminating to get a sense of what it was like for the other. Clients are often amazed at how much information is available energetically by sitting in the chair of the other. (Note, this is not at all appropriate if the other is a perpetrator of trauma or abuse.) At times there may be self-interruptive processes, which the therapist needs to assist the client to work with as they emerge. In the final stage of the task the client returns to their original chair and the therapist and client reflect on the process. Figure 8.6 depicts graphical representation of empty chair work as researched by Les Greenberg. See *Learning Emotion-Focused Therapy* for more detailed accounts of the chair work (Elliott, Watson, et al., 2004).

The power of the empty chair

I would like to share a personal story with you that highlights the power of empty chair work.

I was adopted out as a 10-day-old baby and was told so by my adopted parents when I was 6 years old. They said they chose me! As a curious

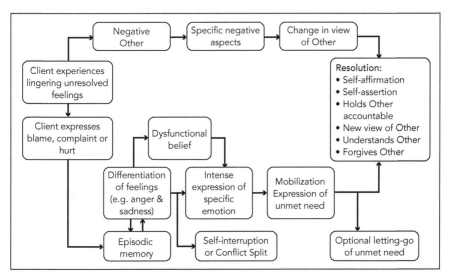

FIGURE 8.6

Steps in empty-chair work for unfinished business. Source Greenberg, et al (1993)

child, I always was interested in knowing who my biological parents were but thought I had to accept the fact that I would never know. But I still hoped. I would be a passenger sitting in the back seat of the car daydreaming and looking up at the clouds. I thought I could see images of my mother in the clouds.

In the early 80s, this all changed. In Victoria, Australia, legislation was passed that adoptees could obtain their original birth certificates. This was despite the fact that the relinquishing mothers never expected to be contacted in the future as they were assured that the files with their details on the original birth certificates were locked away forever.

I was in my mid-20s when I made my application to the organisation that had arranged my adoption. I was keen to understand more about my biological parents, particularly my mother. I had lived in a sort of idealistic bubble, dreaming of the day that I would meet her and the fantastic reunion we would have. I imagined that she would love me completely and that I would meet my wonderful half-brothers and half-sisters. I thought we would all live happily ever after as a big extended family like in the movie *Sound of Music*, which I have seen about 20 times.

For some extraordinary reason, it was thought that putting relinquishing mothers together with adopted children somehow would create a happy ending. Nothing was further from the truth. The people employed in these services were overworked and inexperienced. There was a huge demand on the organisations who had arranged the adoptions. The waiting time blew out to over two years. There was minimal counselling for the adoptees, and often the relinquishing mothers had to cope with receiving unexpected letters or phone calls from organisations that they did not expect to hear from ever again.

My mother was no different. She had been told never to look back and had got on with her life.

At the time of my application, I was provided with rudimentary information about my birth weight, time of birth and physical health. It felt useful to have this information, but by no means was it sufficient. I found out that my biological mother was 23 when she gave birth to me. She was the eldest daughter of three girls. She was well educated and had become a teacher. Her parents were from Ireland and had settled in a very remote part in Western Australia. They were very devout Catholics and the news that their eldest daughter was pregnant created a huge rift in the family. My mother was sent to Melbourne to have me and never returned to live in Western Australia again. She continued to work as a teacher.

I discovered that my biological father was of similar age and they met and had a brief liaison. He was of English origin and a follower of the Church of England faith. Apparently, when he found out that my mother was pregnant, he did offer to marry her but the fact that he was of Church of England faith and she was a Roman Catholic meant that the marriage would be difficult to arrange. My father later believed that my mother had had an abortion.

During the time I was waiting for my application to be finalised, I had my own child, which seemed to accentuate my desire to meet my biological mother. Finally, when he was a few months old, I was contacted by the agency and told my mother would meet me. As you can imagine, I was very excited but also very wary. I had no idea what my mother would be like and whether there was a possibility of an ongoing relationship. I forwarded a detailed letter outlining all the things I wanted to ask her.

At the eleventh hour, my mother changed her mind and refused to meet me. No words can explain the disappointment I was feeling. I am a determined person by nature; some might call me stubborn.

After waiting for over two years, I felt incensed that my request had not been granted. Unfortunately, (and I hate to admit this), but I had no regard for my mother. I thought it was my right to meet her and understand what had happened to me. At the time of this disappointing news, I was listening to a radio announcer. She was known for taking up certain personal requests. I contacted her and asked her whether I could use the radio to reach out to my mother. She felt this was not an appropriate medium but said she knew someone at one of the leading the morning newspapers and perhaps a photo could be taken and published. It might be possible that my mother might recognise me.

So, on one sunny May day in 1986, a newspaper photographer met me in a Melbourne city park and snapped some photos of my son and I. To my surprise, the newspaper liked the photos so much they decided to run it on the *front* page of the paper. It appeared on the Saturday morning before Mother's Day with a headline that read 'a gift of love for lost mother'.

Not surprisingly, when my mother saw it in her local newsagent she was furious. She contacted my social worker and begrudgingly agreed to meet with me. She greeted me with cold disdain. In my attempt to rectify the situation, I asked questions that had been playing on my mind for years. She asked me whether I felt the adoption was a success. I didn't have the heart to tell her it was not. My adopted mother was emotionally distant and neglectful. She told me that she never thought this meeting would occur and was very reticent to give me any information at all. My mother had told no one of my existence. She was very scared that her husband, not my father, who was of Church of England faith, would find out and call her a hypocrite. She had insisted that their children be raised as Catholics. Whilst I understood this in principle, I did not have any understanding of what it was like to suffer the stigma of having an illegitimate child. She was worried I would look for other family members. She agreed to meet me on three occasions in total; two on my own and one with my son. She hardly touched him. At the conclusion of the third meeting, she made it very clear she wanted no contact with me, and I was never to reach out to her again.

I tried to accept that this would be the entire contact with my mother and be happy with that. On my way to work, I would drive past her apartment and was constantly reminded of a dream lost. The yearning for connection did not go away and in fact, probably increased in intensity. I continued to grieve.

Many years later, after my third child was born and I was studying psychology, I began to understand how attachment injuries can have a significant impact on people. The need to legitimise myself was a strong drive.

In 2006, when I was introduced to EFT, I was invited to bring personal material to practice the various interventions we were studying. As the daring person that I am, I had a great idea to use the empty chair technique with the hope of resolving some of the emotional pain of being adopted and not having an ongoing relationship with my biological mother. My practice partner was willing to facilitate the process.

My 'therapist' asked me to imagine my mother was sitting in the other chair opposite me. While I had not seen her for over 20 years and had no physical memory of her, I was asked just to get a sense of her. In the first stages of the session, I was able to 'tell' my mother how unjust and unfair it was that she had given me up. I told how furious I was that she did not want me in her life. This went on for some minutes. After my 'rant' I was able to get in touch with deep grief that had pervaded much of my life. This was a very powerful experience to actually be in contact with the original emotional pain. The therapist then asked me to do something what I thought was quite provocative. She asked me to sit in the chair of my mother. I was curious to understand what this might be like. So, I moved across and sat in what was my 'mother's' chair. I was very surprised as I sat there to become aware of the emptiness that lay inside her. She felt like a shell to me. The facade of 'doing the right thing', being a good Catholic woman and always worried about what other people thought became very apparent to me. In that moment I recognised that there was actually nothing that she would be able to give me. While my life had been hard and challenging, there were many amazing times and experiences. I had learnt to be true to myself. 'What you see is what you get with me.' I never got caught up in the 'what other people think' pressure. I moved back to my own chair, and I become acutely aware that I could now let it go. The yearning that had plagued me my entire life dissipated. I no longer needed or desired contact with her. I was truly free of the attachment trauma that had manifested in emotional pain. It was a remarkable moment that still feels as important today as it did all those years ago.

Chair session with therapist Anne and client Jim

I would like to present another case example. This is a true story but certain facts have been changed and the client has been de-identified, thus given a different name and age. Jim is a 30-year-old gay man who was in a long-term relationship but struggling with intimacy. He found he was keeping himself busy all the time, working long hours in three different jobs, and was exhausted when he gets home. He was curious to understand what that was about. Anne, his middle-aged counsellor, is a competent EFT therapist.

The session began with Jim explaining how this busyness was impacting his life. Jim said that he needed to push himself to get things done. He described that he would become anxious and it was like 'this anxiety train' that took over. When he wasn't anxious, he worried about being in a calm, reflective space because he was 'fearful of what I might think, what might come up'. If he wasn't 'buzzed' he would drink coffee or go looking for things to do to keep himself distracted with 'a million balls in the air … I'm a bee, I can't sit still, I go from flower to flower, I have to work. I'm a worker. I can't sit still'. There was also another voice emerging as Jim spoke; one that said, 'Oh, you're slack, or you know, you're, not doing enough, or you're not using your skills enough'.

Anne explained to Jim that there seems to be a critical voice telling him that he 'should' be busy or that he was slack, and invited him to engage in some two-chair work. She set up four chairs (Stage 1 see Figure 8.1) and invited him to sit in the 'critic' chair (Stage 2). Anne sat beside him. She asked him to say out loud the words he said to himself in his mind, advising, 'Be critical. Can you say what you'd say to yourself?'.

Jim launched into it, addressing the other chair: 'You need to be busy. You can't slack off. Don't slow down. If you look like you're not doing anything then you're not doing your job. Yeah, the busier you are the better you are'.

He hesitated, and Anne enquired as to what was happening. Then he said, 'Don't go there, don't feel … even if you think you need to say something, don't say it. You're going to stuff it up. You're feeling too much, too emotional. Suck it up, princess'. He seemed to falter. 'I don't want that to destroy what we've got going on. Everything that we've built so far. Even though you've got good intentions, you know full well that you could wreck it'.

Anne asked Jim to swap chairs and asked him what it was like to hear that barrage. Jim sat for a moment and acknowledged that he agreed with the other side. He stated that he thought that side knew what he was doing, was determined to get things done and this side 'just had to tag along ... just has to shut up'.

Anne re-emphasised Jim's words: 'Shut up ... you are right ...'.

Jim said, 'It's not completely right ... I would be more in tune with who I am if you would shut the fuck up and ... let me speak'.

Jim felt sad because he knew the other side would never give him what he needed. 'I need love and appreciation,' he explained. 'I need someone who understands me emotionally, and can be in my space, and support me ... this side needs to be able to speak.'

Anne asked Jim what happens when that side shuts you up.

'I lose myself,' he replied, 'Am I really being me? Or am I being this ... a busy version of myself?'

Anne asked Jim to look at the 'self' sitting in the other chair opposite him. He explained that he had known that part for a long time — 'forever ... it's not recent'. Anne asked him to get a sense when this started and he replied, 'I've always been told, by Mum, that I'm the sensitive one ... the sensitive boy.'

Anne noticed emotion arising as Jim began to say more (self-interruptive process). She urged him to stay with the experience and she invited his mother into the other chair (Stage 2 empty-chair work). He found this confronting.

'She always used to say that 'I just need you to have a ... dad figure... to go camping'. Jim gestured a 'gung-ho' action with his fist and arm. Anne copied his gesture and mirrored the sentiment 'to be more of a man'.

Jim's father left the family when he was very young. Jim was the youngest child of four children and his three elder siblings were sisters. His mother saw that he was sensitive, quiet and didn't speak up, but still thought he needed to be more of a man. Jim was quite distressed as he told Anne, 'She didn't fight for me'. He recalled leaning to drive and the female instructor yelling at him. 'I literally wanted to stop at the traffic lights, get out of the car and run away'. At the end of the lesson Jim 'bawled my eyes out, told Mum … she forced me to go back and deal with this woman … who apologised but …'.

He needed his mother to go and say to the woman, 'My son needs you to be respectful'.

At a very young age, Jim had been part of a fundamentalist church. He was nurtured and mentored by one of the ministers. When he came out as gay he was rejected by the ministers and the church. No one talked to him about it and, most painfully, his family continued to attend the church.

'There was no one there for me,' he told Anne. Jim's mother was always busy. She took on many foster children and the household was often in chaos. Jim said, 'It was a joke — the amount of love for other people and the amount of shit-storms that she was putting out, and not a whole lot of time for me.'

He found that being busy was a way of avoiding all the drama. And his mother was the role model of busyness: 'This is what you do — keep busy, take care of other people, shut up and don't say anything, be strong.'

Jim needed his mother 'to understand my feeling and my sensitive self … she's just not getting it'. His request was highly unlikely to be fulfilled, and Anne challenged him to 'let go of the need of wanting' his mother's approval. He replied:

> I used to see her as very strong, and I used to see her as very wise, but I don't actually see that anymore. Now it's kind of turning into … there's a bit of disdain, there's a bit of disgust around this persona of strength, and this persona of wise … and of doing stuff for other people. But I actually see the situation as quite fucked up. I need to distance myself; I need to push that part of you away from me, because it's really quite horrible. It's quite, it's quite disgusting how she puts on this face of love, and puts on this face of genuine Christian care. But in actual underneath there's quite a lot of judgement … not true to herself.

Jim felt loved by his mother but his sensitivity was not valued, nor did he feel protected by her. He began to get angry, 'I feel cheated that I lived up to that, because now, looking back at her, it's actually all a lie.' He directed his anger towards her:

> It's actually all a lie, how you tried to sell being good, and tried to sell
> being nice to other people, and caring for other people, when in actual
> fact, there was a lot of shit that you did. There was this disgust ... in that
> it was fake, you kind of cheated me, in what you set out for me.

Anne suggested that, 'It leaves you in the position where you keep on trying, that there is no end to it ... you will never truly be able to please everybody completely.'

It was important for Jim to let go of the need for his mother's validation. He said, 'I don't need your validation. I don't need to look up to you and see me doing good as something that you would appreciate ... you can go back to the fucken country.' Jim laughed. Anne asked his mother to 'leave'.

Anne invited Jim to swap chairs (now identified as the adaptive critic — Stage 3) and asked him, 'What's here now?'

He described this self in this chair as the 'thinking' part. Anne asked the 'thinking part' what he thought of the self sitting opposite. 'He's so strong,' Jim said. 'When I first started, I kind of saw this side [he pointed to the opposite chair] as kind of a younger me, a smaller me that was too gentle, too soft, but I actually see this side now as kind of a gentle strength.'

Anne suggested that Jim's sensitivity was one of his greatest strengths, and he acknowledged this, saying, 'This side kind of gives it coffee, gives it ... busy ... trying to water it down.'

Anne said she wondered, 'What now?'

'Time to start trusting you more, even if I don't want to hear it ... not be in the background.'

Anne told Jim to swap chairs and asked him what it felt like now that part could see him. 'It feels good,' he replied. 'Part of me has been actually thinking if what I'm doing right now isn't what I really want to do. And I don't know whether it's that side being anxious or whatever, but I think I've lost a sense of genuineness and a sense of being authentic — which this side really values ... I'm not sure what it looks like without the buzz, that's the interesting thing, there's this ... what does that even look like?'

Anne encouraged Jim to ask what he needed from the other side. 'I need you to motivate me,' he said. 'I need you to rationalise things for me, but don't over [do it], don't keep ... don't lose sight of me, because I know what the fuck I need, and I, … this side's integrity and this side's sense of me, is really important …'.

They swapped chairs. Jim said, 'It scares me a little bit, but this side knows that that side is authentic and genuine and it's okay to be scared. Because that side is there … he's a good part, he's definitely got me to where I am, and definitely, I do appreciate you, I do value your input, but not you taking over.'

In EFT it's important to start a task and finish with the same task. The session started with a conflict split, worked through interruptive processes and engaged in empty chair with Jim's mother and Jim as a young man. It was necessary as a way of finishing the task to go back to the conflict split process. Anne asked Jim to go back to the critical chair (Stage 3). As he sat there, he described things as feeling very different. There was less critical-ness. The therapist asked how this side felt, having heard and witnessed what the experiencing self had endured. Jim felt more compassion for the experiencing self and had more understanding. He also knew that being busy was a way to protect himself from his mother's unavailability. The experiencing self was relieved that the critic, now more accurately described as the adaptive critic, was less harsh and had softened. There was a willing-ness to work together. The adaptive critic would be more gentle in offering suggestions and the experiencing self was more prepared to listen and be guided. Jim needed both these aspects to work together. The experiencing self wanted to be seen and less hidden.

After a series of chair swaps, the sides reached agreement. Jim com-mented on how hard it was to know which chair was which. This was a sign that integration had occurred. Jim was invited to return to his original chair (Stage 4) and reflect on the process. He was amazed at what had emerged and commented that there was a great deal to think about. Anne was aware that the meaning-making of the session would be likely to occur outside the session, because Jim was still processing what had actually occurred. It is really important to allow the client to make sense and meaning in their own time. It is very easy for therapists to be eager to join the dots for the client, but this may actually be disempowering.

Follow-up comment by Jim:

> The session with Anne was quite a challenge for me emotionally and mentally. I have had the issue of this drive to 'keep busy' for a long time,

and for the most part it has been useful in motivating me and pushing me towards goals — but this became too much. In the start of the session, Anne encouraged me to start talking from this voice, which became jarring for me, receiving that message in the opposite chair. It was confronting to see this as coming from my mother, as I have always viewed her as strong and dedicated in helping others, but it never occurred to me how damaging this was to me growing up. This experience of neglecting my emotions as a way of coping and seeing my 'sensitive self' as different hit a real chord of not being cared for in the way I needed. This insight unpacked my own views of myself that started when I was quite young. It was a big revelation to see my emotional side as being strong and to recognise that I truly needed this part.

After the session it was like my brain was recalibrating a new way of looking at things. I was able to name emotions and be brutally honest with myself on how I felt on a day-to-day basis. Also, the busy voice is still around but it has less power and I can see through it as being unrealistic and unfair to my needs.

The battle with this voice is more easily won and I am more confident with just being present with my emotions. I think I have a deeper trust in my gut and I see value in tuning into this side of me more often.

Chair work is a very helpful method for working with intrapsychic issues such as internal conflict, self-interruption, and unfinished business. The main issue when working with people with significant emotional pain as a result of trauma is that the client must feel safe enough intra-psychically to work in the chairs. Clients who dissociate may not even be aware of it, and therefore it is important to identify the client's ability to be embodied before engaging in chair work. The method of grounding and safe place is highlighted in Chapter 6. If the client is not able to move in and out of dissociative states it is not prudent to engage in chair work.

Chapter 9

Conclusion:
A meta-perspective and how
people come to live an aware life

So, as a way to complete this book, let's look at emotional pain and healing from a different, more 'meta' perspective. I have watched many of my clients enter therapy, reduce their symptoms significantly and function better, only to find themselves feeling alienated from family and friends, and not necessarily feeling part of their group or community anymore. Initially this puzzled me; I had thought psychological health would render them more able to 'fit in' to society, not feel separate from it. What I concluded was that as we individuate and become our true selves — what I see as *true* healing — we no longer 'fit' into a group mentality.

Humans are interesting creatures, in that we are part of our community and need it in order to feel safe, but we also need to feel individuated. Our Western society bases too much on the idea of individuation and meeting individual needs, whereas Eastern cultures emphasise the needs of the community over the individual. In my opinion, to be a fully adaptive, functioning human, we need both. We need to function as an individual in a community that values both individuation and group identity. The individual needs to have integrity, good intention for self and other, intuition, insight, and be integrated so they can foster interrelatedness and be inclusive of diversity. These qualities need to be integrated not merely as concepts, but as lived and embodied characteristics of the individual in society.

The following theory emerged out of my client work and various readings and discussions with others. Please feel free to accept or reject this view. It is presented as an attempt to make sense of our complicated existence.

The sex, drugs and rock'n'roll box

Most people live in a state of unconsciousness. We get wrapped up in what society deems important, by looking a particular way, living a particular lifestyle, and purchasing the latest and the greatest — 'Keeping up with the Joneses', as my mother and her generational peers would say. We get caught up in the fast pace of life and must have the most up-to-date technology.

Most of us live in this state without even realising there could be an alternative. Sometimes there is a sense that something is missing, but it's hard to work out what it is. We seem to have everything, and everyone else seems to be okay with their lives and how things are. We may ask ourselves: 'What's wrong with me that I feel so alone, different, or misunderstood?'. We feel overwhelmed with the busyness of our lives and the pressures we find ourselves under at work and at home. We tend to value busyness as a social signal that indicates our importance and success. People resort to activities that keep them numb to the feelings of discomfort and overwhelm that follow. Using recreational drugs or alcohol, over-eating or under-eating, and porn and sex overindulgence are all ways of coping with the unhappiness. We are sold the idea that the remedy for unhappiness is pharmacological, so we go to the doctor, who prescribes antidepressants. Often this adds to the problem by adding shame to the equation. Focusing on the external becomes a preoccupation. We might say: 'I am not getting my needs met; it must be someone's fault'. We live in a type of bubble or box, like that shown in Figure 9.1. I call it the 'sex, drugs and rock'n'roll box'.

I am certainly not saying that sex, drugs, or rock'n'roll are all bad, or even mostly bad. What I *am* saying is that how we use them can be problematic.

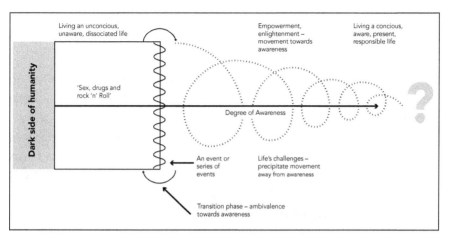

FIGURE 9.1

The 'sex, drugs and rock'n'roll box'.

This box has boundaries or edges that we know instinctively and that give us the feeling that somehow, we are safe and in control. It's desirable to be in the box, because that's where everybody is. We want to belong. We do everything to stay there. Instant gratification lives in the box. Denial and avoidance live in the box. While in the box, we don't have to be responsible for ourselves or how we treat others. It's all about 'me! me! me!'. We have been told that the world is meant to be for us to have fun and be happy. We live in a kind of mindless void where everything is geared towards being happy in a rather selfish and hedonistic way. We are judgemental of those who are different and live outside the box. Even contemplating that there could be something else outside the box, or to consider living out of the box, creates a sense of uncertainly and fearfulness. We live in a state of dissociation.

Dissociation is like daydreaming. Children daydream all the time. It's something they do when they are bored, shy, or tired. It enables them to go to places in their imaginations where life is colourful, interesting, safe and happy. When a child is fearful, daydreaming can be used to create a happy place. Dissociation becomes problematic when a child loses the sense of present reality and withdraws from the world. When a child experiences trauma or abuse, dissociation is a very effective coping mechanism, but it becomes problematic when they no longer engage with others or lose a sense of what's real. Ongoing dissociation in children can later lead to difficulties in learning and engaging in appropriate relationships. There is often a sense of not being quite present to the 'here-and-now' or experiencing a sense of numbness or other out-of-body-type sensations.

Dissociation is an extension of the fight/flight response, which is an adaptive and normal response to fear. We all experience a physiological response when we are frightened. From an evolutionary perspective, animals in the wild operate from this system as a means of survival. Knowing when to stay and fight for one's territory or kin or when to flee is a very important part of our survival instinct. An example of freezing is when the antelope plays dead. The lion knows only fresh kill is safe to eat, as an old carcass may be potentially rancid or poisonous. We as humans have a similar innate mechanism, but we have no lions to flee from. The mechanism that operates when we can't flee or fight is dissociation. Our flight/fight mechanism gets activated when we feel danger. Anxiety is a chronic form of fear.

Dissociation can become habitual when the world seems unengaging or threatening. It can sometimes come from a desire to be invisible or not wanting to be around. In order to be present to the here-and-now you need to become mindful and body aware. You need to be grounded in your body. This enables you to be fully cognisant of your surroundings and can assist you to make appropriate judgements of what immediate action to take and what to do next. Often being present to the here-and-now involves a choice. You can choose to be grounded in your body and present to your sensations, thoughts and emotions. For those who are fearful and have used dissociation as a means of protection, they need to feel safe as well as making a choice to be present. They need to break the habit of dissociation and develop a new habit of groundedness, embodiment, and presence.

There has been a great deal written about the functions of the two hemispheres of the brain. The left brain is apparently where we use logic and rationality to make sense of our world. The right brain is thought to be where our creativity lies. Thinking outside the square, or laterally, is a characteristic of the right brain. Often only the left brain is well developed and people get stuck in their 'thinking' brain. Our society encourages us to learn in a very linear fashion. Our education system is an excellent example of this — children who don't have a sequential learning style really struggle. We actually need to have both parts of our brain functioning equally well. The creative part of our brain enables us to understand the world as a vast and varied system full of diversity and wonderment. Our intuition comes from a combination of working with our right brain and our embodied knowledge. It's like the head and the heart working together; integration of mind and body. We need to learn to trust knowledge other than logic and science. We are confronted with so much we don't know. We need the strengths of both hemispheres to find a way out of the box.

How to get out of the box

But how do we get out of the box, and what's on the other side? Sometimes something terrible happens to us. We might lose our job, a good friend or a family member dies, or our health deteriorates and we may be forced to look at the world differently. This often requires self-reflection or maybe therapy. But it takes conscious effort and considerable time. For some the avoidance strategies remain and life continues as before. For others, a questioning begins. You begin to question your life and the people in it. The wiggly grey dotted line on Figure 9.1 represents this transition phase. People describe this as seeing things clearly for the first time, or that somehow a veil has lifted. There is a sense of liberation from constraints of what everyone else does. A sense of finding oneself and being 'true' to themselves. There is a sense of movement, awareness and fulfilment. A lot of those self-help books actually start to make sense.

Unfortunately, many of your friends don't understand your new view of the world and the people who live outside the box. You begin to feel alienated but in a different way. This alienation is not like before when you were in the box, because now you at least feel as if you are 'on the right path'. The interesting thing about this path is that you are not really sure what's at the other end. What is it that you are striving for and working so hard to get to? Some people call it enlightenment or self-actualisation. Some people call it heaven, nirvana or bliss. You can get a sense a *flow,* as described by Csikszentmihalyi (2002) and, if open to it, synchronicity can guide us. I am not really sure exactly what it is but I do know it's something that has motivated me my whole life. Many human beings are guided by this and motivated by this drive. Personally, I have worked hard to strive to know more. Ironically, the more I know the less I know. Wisdom in its true sense is humbling.

For many who have ventured cautiously out of the box, there is a strong temptation to go back into the box — and the arrows on Figure 9.1 show this movement back and forth. There comes a time, however, when there is no going back. Going back to being mindless and ignorant becomes impossible. It's often a lonely path and you might lose friends along the way. New ones certainly appear as you begin to become discerning about who you can trust your sharings with and who you can't.

The journey forward is not without its challenges. I naively thought that being out of the box and feeling liberated was the end of the story. This is definitely not the case. What begins to happen is a series of cycles (see Figure 9.1) that can feel like what is sometimes existentially and poetically described as 'the dark night of the soul' or parts of the 'hero's journey'. We enter challenging periods of life where things no longer run smoothly, and we are forced to look at ourselves and our behaviours. As we go into the dip of the cycle, depression, anxiety and distress may emerge. As we navigate our way through these difficult times, we gather strength and knowledge about ourselves that may not have been a present before. As a cycle ends, things slowly improve and we feel empowered and more enlightened. We may even get a sense that we have moved further along that path. However, life has a habit of throwing further challenges our way, and we may find ourselves some months later faced with work, personal, or spiritual crises. As seen in Figure 9.1, the intensity and scale of the challenges lessens over time. An awareness that a cycle is emerging and recognition that something is learned through each cycle helps to lessen the strength of the distress. We develop resilience.

An interesting distinction for those who find their way out of the box is coming across people who 'get it' and those who don't. Those who 'get it' may have navigated their way out of the box by journeying through it but there are some people who have experienced life without ever really being in the box. They arrive already sitting on the grey wiggly line. They see world quite differently from their parents, siblings and friends. Often there is one child born into or adopted into a family who is distinctly unlike the other family members. Their level of sensitivity is often commented on. These children may be *highly sensitive* (as seen in Chapter 4) to their surroundings, are deeply empathic, and have almost an instinctual way of experiencing the world. They are deeply affected by nature and have wisdom beyond their years. They often realise there is something different about them and feel alienated and alone in a really deep sense as they feel outcast by their family and friends. Their families may ostracise them for all sorts of reasons but primarily because they are different. They may be blamed for the family's difficulties and scapegoated. This child is left feeling confused and encumbered with a sense that it is all their fault. They lose a sense of who they are and a connection to their 'truth'. Such children can be the target of all kinds of abuse. They grow up questioning everything, but often, they get stuck along the way. It is likely the child will either internalise or externalise the blame or guilt. Internalising forces the child to turn inward, become withdrawn, and unwell. Externalising causes outward-directed behaviours, projections, blaming of others, and sometimes aggressiveness and hyper-activity. Both can be present in any individual. If they are lucky enough, they will meet others who have navigated their way out of the box or are like them, and begin to feel validated so that they might renew their motivation to follow their 'truth' again. These highly sensitive children grow up into highly sensitive adults, but this sensitivity needs to be seen as an asset, not a curse. Part of coming to know oneself and being more comfortable in one's own skin is valuing such qualities as sensitivity. It is estimated that twenty per cent of our population is made up of these highly sensitive people.

The other end of the arrow — the dark side of humanity

And what's at the other end of the continuum? The extreme end of dissociation or unawareness is where people have lost compassion for others. This is where our psychopaths, dictators and paedophiles live. These people have, for whatever reason, lost the ability to care how their actions might impact others. Their level of dissociation is so extreme that there is no room for consideration of others and their sole purpose in life is control and survival. It's like 'kill or be killed'. Coercion, violence and evil lives here. There may be a context around how these people came to be this way but their recovery is doubtful. We can have compassion for their plight but often the devastation that they create leaves a trail of destruction and misery in its wake.

Living out of the box

So you have found yourself partly out of the box. You choose to be more aware. You choose to take care of yourself. You don't want to be unconscious with alcohol and other drugs. You don't over-eat or under-eat. You want meaningful relationships not just sex or porn. You leave your dead-end job and take an active part in your life and career choices. You leave an unsatisfactory relationship. Colours seem brighter and people more real. Life is often more exciting and emotions felt more acutely. Relationships are more vibrant but can be more painful. Your awareness is more perceptive and there is a sense that there is more to life than what you can see, hear and taste. You recognise you have to be more responsible and grown-up. You identify that you can't change anyone else except yourself. You learn to become more tolerant of others and less judgmental. You learn to stop blaming and complaining. You start to live a more aware life. You begin to change. You learn to be mindful of the impact you have on others. You choose to be respectful with every person to person interaction. You recognise the role of responsibility in taking care of yourself, your community and the planet.

By living an aware life, you chose to change yourself, and the flow-on effect of that is that you can change the world one person at a time. If each person you meet is positively impacted by you enough to be inspired to choose to exit the box, they too will change their lives, and so might the people they meet, and on and so on. That way we all choose to live more aware lives and ultimately, we could change the world and there would be less suffering.

By way of finishing, allow me to share another personal story. In 1983, I was 23. This was during the Cold War and nuclear armament was a hot topic. I considered myself an environmentalist even back then. There were marches in the city demanding nuclear disarmament. As I was walking through the streets of Melbourne with hundreds of people, I realised that as an individual I was quite powerless to make any significant change. This saddened me. During the years that followed I have researched and studied alternative health, became a vegetarian, and engaged in Eastern spiritual practices as a way of trying to make a difference. I began to realise that I had little impact on changing the masses, but if I worked on changing myself, that in turn had the potential to change the quality of relationships I had around me — which may in turn catalyse change in the broader community. When I began my psychology training it further occurred to me that as a psychotherapist, I had the potential to influence and facilitate change in individuals, one person at a time.

Now, as an EFT trainer, I have taught other psychologists, counsellors and psychotherapists how to assist people to work through the emotional pain. Finding safe and efficient ways to support people work through and liberate themselves from their emotional woundedness has become my life's work. Writing this book is an expansion of that commitment. So this book, which is the culmination of my life's experiences so far, both personal and professional, is my gift to you and I hope you might apply the principles contained within these pages and are able to take something from it both personally and professionally. Take care.

Melissa

References

Preface

Dolhanty, J., & Greenberg, L.S. (2007). Emotion-focused therapy in the treatment of eating disorders. *European Psychotherapy, 7*, 97–116.

Dolhanty, J., & Greenberg, L.S. (2009). Emotion-focused therapy in a case of anorexia nervosa. *Clinical Psychology and Psychotherapy, 16*, 336–382.

Dolhanty, J., & Lafrance, A. (2019). Emotion-focused therapy for eating disorders. In L.S. Greenberg & R.N. Goldman (Eds.), *Clinical handbook of Emotion-focused therapy* (pp. 403–424). Washington, DC: American Psychological Association.

Elliott, R.K., & Shahar, B. (2017). Emotion-focused therapy for social anxiety (EFT-SA). *Person-Centred & Experiential Psychotherapies, 16*, 140–158.

Janov, A. (1973). *The primal scream: Primal therapy: The cure for neurosis.* New York, NY: Abacus.

Paivio, S.C., & Pascual-Leone, A. (2010). *Emotion-focused therapy for complex trauma: An integrative approach.* Washington, DC: American Psychological Association

Shahar, B., Bar-Kalifa, E., & Alon, E. (2017). Emotion-focused therapy for social anxiety disorder. *Journal of Consulting and Clinical Psychology, 85*, 238–249.

Warwar, S.H., Links, P.S., Greenberg, L.S., & Bergmans, Y. (2008). Emotion-focused principles for working with borderline personality disorder. *Journal of Psychiatric Practice, 14*, 94–104.

Watson, J.C., & Greenberg, L.S. (2017). *Emotion-focused therapy for generalized anxiety.* Washington, DC: American Psychological Association

Watson, J.C., Timulak, L., & Greenberg, L.S. (2019). Emotion-focused therapy for generalized anxiety disorder. In L. S. Greenberg & R. N. Goldman (Eds.), *Clinical handbook of emotion-focused therapy* (pp. 315–336). Washington, DC: American Psychological Association.

Chapter 1

Briere, J.N., & Scott, C. (2014). *Principles of trauma therapy: A guide to symptoms, evaluation, and treatment* (DSM-5 Update). Thousand Oaks, CA: SAGE.

Herman, J L. (1993). Complex PTSD: A syndrome in survivors of prolonged and repeated trauma. *Journal of Traumatic Stress, 5*, 377–391.

Ogden, P. (2006). *Trauma and the body: A sensorimotor approach to psychotherapy*. New York, NY: Norton.

Ogden, P., & Fisher, J. (2015). *Sensorimotor psychotherapy: Interventions for trauma and attachment*. New York, NY: Norton.

Paivio, S.C., & Pascual-Leone, A. (2010). *Emotion-focused therapy for complex trauma: An integrative approach*. Washington, DC: American Psychological Association.

Rothschild, B. (2011). *Trauma essentials: The go-to guide (go-to guides for mental health)* London, England: Norton.

Timulak, L. (2015). *Transforming emotional pain in psychotherapy: An emotion-focused approach*. East Sussex, England: Routledge.

van der Kolk, B.A. (1993). Biological considerations about emotions, trauma, memory, and the brain. In S. Ablon, D. Brown, E. Khantzian, & J.E. Mack (Eds.), *Human feelings: Exploration in affect development and meaning* (pp. 221–240). Hillsdale, NJ: Analytic Press.

van der Kolk, B.A. (1994). The body keeps the score: Memory and the evolving psychobiology of posttraumatic stress. *Harvard Review of Psychiatry, 1,* 253–265.

van der Kolk, B.A. (1995). The body, memory, and the psychobiology of trauma. In A.J. Alpert (Ed.), *Sexual abuse recalled: Treating trauma in the ear of the recovered memory debate* (pp. 29–60). Northvale, NJ: Jason Aronson.

van der Kolk, B.A. (2005). Developmental trauma disorder. *Psychiatric Annals, 35,* 401–408.

van der Kolk, B.A., & Fisler, R.E. (1994). Childhood abuse and neglect and loss of self-regulation. *Bulletin of the Menninger Clinic, 58,* 145–168.

Chapter 2

American Psychiatric Association. (2000). *Diagnostic and statistical manual of mental disorders* (4th ed., text rev.). Washington, DC: Author

American Psychiatric Association. (2013). *Diagnositc and statistical manual of mental disorders* (5th ed.). Washington, DC: Author.

Bryant, R.A. (2012). Simplifying complex PTSD: Comment on Resick et al. (2012). *Journal of Traumatic Stress, 25*, 252–253.

Cloitre, M., Miranda, R., Stovall-McClough, K.C., & Han, H. (2005). Beyond PTSD: Emotion-regulation and interpersonal porblems as predictors of functional impairment in survivors of childhood abuse. *Behavior Therapy, 36,* 119–124.

Connor, P., & Higgins, D.J. (2008). The 'HEALTH' model — Part 2: Case study of a guideline-based treatment program for Complex PTSD relating to childhood sexual abuse. *Sexual and Relationship Therapy, 23*, 401–140.

Department of Veteran Affairs. (n.d.). Case study — posttraumtic stress disorder. Retrieved from http://at-ease.dva.gov.au/veterans/resources/case-studies/case-study-ptsd/

Friedman, M.J. (2013). Finalizing PTSD in DSM-5: Getting here from there and where to go next. *Journal of Traumatic Stress, 26*, 548–556.

Friedman, M.J., Resik, P.A., Bryant, R.A., & Brewin, C.R. (2011). Considering PTSD for DSM-5. *Depression and Anxiety, 28*, 750–769.

Goodman, M. (2012). Complex PTSD is on the trauma spectrum: Comment on Resick et al. (2012). *Journal of Traumatic Stress, 25*, 254–255.

Herman, J.L. (1992). Complex PTSD: A syndrome in survivors of porlonged and repeated trauma. *Journal of Traumatic Stress, 5*, 377–391.

Herman, J.L. (2012). CPTSD is a distinct entity: Comment on Resick et al. (2012). *Jounal of Traumatic Stress, 25*, 256–257.

Lindauer, R.J.L. (2012). Child maltreatment — Clinical PTSD diagnosis not enough?!: Comment on Resick et al. (2012). *Jounal of Traumatic Stress, 25*, 258–259.

Resick, P.A., Bovin, M.J., Calloway, A.L., Dick, A.M., King, M.W., Mitchell, K.S., … Wolf, E.J. (2012). A critical evaluation of the complex PTSD literature: Implications for DSM-5. *Journal of Traumatic Stress, 25*, 241–251.

Rothschild, B. (2000). *The body remembers: The psychophysiology of trauma and trauma treatment.* New York, NY: Norton.

van der Kolk, B.A. (2005). Developmental trauma disorder: Toward a reational dignosis for childrne with comple trauma histories *Psychiatric Annals, 35*, 401–408.

van der Kolk, B.A. (2007). The history of trauma in psychiatry. In M.J. Friedman, T.M. Keane, & P.A. Resick (Eds.), *Handbook of PTSD: Science and Practice*. New York, NY: Guilford Press

Chapter 3

Bechara, A., (2004). The role of emotion in decision-making: Evidence from neurological patients with orbitofrontal damage. *Brain and Cognition, 55,* 30–40.

Bowlby, J. (1973). *Attachment and loss, Vol. 2: Separation: Anxiety and anger.* New York, NY: Basic Books.

Bowlby, J. (1988). *A secure base: Parent-child attachment and heathy human development.* New York, NY: Basic Books.

Cooper, M.L., Shaver, P.R., & Collins, N.L. (1998). Attachment styles, emotion regulation, and adjustment in adolescence. *Journal of Personality and Social Psychology, 74,* 1380–1397.

Ekman, P. (1972). *Darwin and facial expression: A century of research in review.* New York, NY: Academic Press.

Elliott, R.K., Greenberg, L.S., & Lietaer, G. (2004). Research on experiential psychotherapies. In M.J. Lambert, A.E. Bergin, & S.L. Garfield (Eds.), *Handbook of psychotherapy and behavior change* (5th ed., pp. 493–539). New York, NY: Wiley.

Elliott, R.K., Watson, J.C., Goldman, R.N., & Greenberg, L.S. (2004). *Learning emotion-focused therapy: The process-experiential approach to change.* Washington, DC: American Psychological Association.

Greenberg, L.S., Rice, L.N., & Elliott, R.K. (1993). *Facilitating emotional change: The moment-by-moment process.* New York, NY: Guilford Press.

Greenberg, L.S., & Safran, J.D. (1989). Emotion in psychology, *American Psychologist, 44,* 19–29.

Izard, C.E. (1977). *Human emotions.* New York, NY: Plenum Press.

Izard, C.E. (2010). The many meanings/aspects of emotion: Definitions, functions, activation, and regulation. *Emotion Review, 2,* 363–370.

James, W. (1884). What is an emotion? *Mind, 9,* 188–205.

LeDoux, J. (1996). *The emotional brain: The mysterious underpinnings of emotional life.* New York, NY: Simon & Schuster.

Paivio, S.C., & Pascual-Leone, A. (2010). *Emotion-focused therapy for complex trauma: An integrative approach.* Washington, DC: American Psychological Association

Pennebaker, J.W. (1990). *Opening up: The healing power of confiding in others.* New York, NY: William Morrow.

Chapter 4

Aron, E. (1996). *The highly sensitive person: How to thrive when the world overwhelms you.* NY: Harper Collins.

Chapter 5

Arntz, A. (2012). Imagery re-scripting as a therapeutic technique: Review of clinical trials, basic studies, and research agenda. *Journal of Experimental Psychopathology, 3,* 189–208.

Arntz, A. (2015). Imagery Rescripting for Posttraumatic Stress Disorder. In N.C. Thoma & D. McKay (Eds.), *Working with emotion in cognitive–behavioural therapy: Techniques for clinical practice* (pp. 203–215). New York, NY: Guilford Press.

Beck, A.T. (1996). Beyond belief: A therapy of modes, personality and psychopathology In P.M. Salkovskis (Ed.), *Frontiers of cognitive therapy* (pp. 1–25). New York, NY: Guilford Press.

Berry, (2015) personal communication

Elliott, R.K., Greenberg, L.S., & Lietaer, G. (2004). Research on experiential psychotherapies. In M.J. Lambert, A.E. Bergin, & S.L. Garfield (Eds.), *Handbook of psychotherapy and behavior change* (5th ed., pp. 493–539). New York, NY: Wiley.

Elliott, R.K., Slatick, E., & Urman, M. (2001). Qualitative change process research on psychotherapy: Alternative strategies. In J. Frommer & D.L. Rennie (Eds.), *Qualitative psychotherapy research: Methods and methodology* (pp. 69–111). Lengerich, Germany: Pabst.

Elliott, R.K., Watson, J.C., Goldman, R.N., & Greenberg, L.S. (2004). *Learning emotion-focused therapy: The process-experiential approach to change.* Washington, DC: American Psychological Association.

Gendlin, E.T. (1981). *Focusing* (2nd ed.). Toronto: Bantum Books.

Gendlin, E.T. (1996). *Focusing-oriented psychotherapy: A manual of the experinetial method.* New York, NY: Routledge.

Greenberg, L.S. (2002). *Emotion-focused therapy: Coaching clients to work through their feelings.* Washington, DC: American Psychological Association.

Greenberg, L.S. (2004). Emotion-focused therapy. *Clinical Psychology and Psychotherapy, 11,* 3–16.

Greenberg, L.S. (2010, February). *The transforming power of emotions in individual and couple therapy.* Paper presented at the Emotion Focused Therapy Workshop in dialogue with IEFT, Sydney.

Greenberg, L.S. (2011). *Emotion focused therapy.* Washington, DC: American Psychological Association

Greenberg, L.S., Elliott, R.K., & Pos, A. (2007). Emotion-focused therapy: An overview *European Psychotherapy, 7,* 19–39.

Greenberg, L.S., & Paivio, S.C. (1997). *Working with emotions in psychotherapy.* New York, NY: The Guilford Press.

Greenberg, L.S., Rice, L.N., & Elliott, R.K. (1993). *Facilitating emotional change: The moment-by-moment process.* New York, NY: Guilford Press.

Greenberg, L.S., & Watson, J.C. (1998). Experiential therapy of depression: Differential effects of client-centered relationship conditions and process experiential interventions. *Psychotherapy Research, 8,* 210–224.

Greenberg, L.S., & Watson, J.C. (2006). *Emotion-focused therapy for depression.* Washington, DC: American Psychological Association.

Greenberg, L.S., Watson, J.C., & Lietaer, G. (Eds.). (1998). *Handbook of experiential psychotherapy.* New York, NY: Guilford Press

Lane, R.D., Ryan, L., Nadel, L., & Greenberg, L. (2015). Memory reconsolidation, emotional arousal, and the process of change in psychotherapy: New insights from brain science. *Behavioural and Brain Sciences, 38,* 1–64.

Le Doux, J. (1996). The emotional brain: The mysterious underpinnings of emotional life. New York, NY: Simon & Schuster.

Paivio, S.C., & Pascual-Leone, A. (2010). *Emotion-focused therapy for complex trauma: An integrative approach.* Washington, DC: American Psychological Association

Perls, F., Hefferline, R.F., & Goodman, P. (1951). *Gestalt therapy.* New York, NY: Dell.

Ricard, M. (2015). Altruism: The power of compassion to change yourself and the world London, England: Atlantic Books.

Singer, T., & Klimecki, O.M. (2014). Empathy and compassion. Current Biology, 24, R875-R878.

Vygotsky, L.S. (1978). *Mind in society: the development of higher psychological processes*. Cambridge, MA: Harvard University Press.

Watson, J.C., & Greenberg, L.S. (2017). *Emotion focused therapy for generalized anxiety*. Washington, DC: American Psychological Association

Watson, J.C., Greenberg, L.S., & Lietaer, G. (1998). The experiential paradigm unfolding. In L.S. Greenberg, J.C. Watson, & G. Lietaer (Eds.), *Handbook of experiential psychotherapy* (pp. 3–27). New York, NY: Guilford Press.

Zajonc, R.B. (2000). Feeling and thinking: Closing the debate over the interpendence of affect. In J.P. Forgas (Ed.), *Feeling and thinking: The role of affect in social cognition* (pp. 31–58). New York, NY: Cambridge University Press.

Chapter 6

American Psychiatric Association. (2013). *Diagnostic and statistical manual of mental disorders* (5th ed.). Washington, DC: Author.

Arntz, A. (2012). Imagery rescripting as a therapeutic technique: Review of clinical trials, basic studies, and research agenda. *Journal of Experimental Psychopathology, 3,* 189–208.

Arntz, A. (2015). Imagery rescripting for posttraumatic stress disorder. In N.C. Thoma & D. McKay (Eds.), *Working with emotion in cognitive–behavioural therapy: Techniques for clinical practice* (pp. 203–215). New York, NY: Guilford Press.

Carryer, J.R., & Greenberg, L.S. (2010). Optimal levels of emotional arousal in experiential therapy of depression. *Journal of Consulting and Clinical Psychology, 78,* 190–199.

Ekman, P. (1972). *Darwin and facial expression: A century of research in review*. New York, NY: Academic Press.

Elliott, R.K., Watson, J.C., Goldman, R.N., & Greenberg, L.S. (2004*). Learning emotion-focused therapy: The process-experiential approach to change*. Washington, DC: American Psychological Association.

Ford, J.D. (2009). Neurobiological and developmental research: Clinical implications. In C.A. Courtois & J.D. Ford (Eds.), *Treating complex traumatic stress disorders: An evidence based guide* (pp. 31–58). New York, NY: Guilford Press.

Gendlin, E.T. (1981). *Focusing* (2nd ed.). Toronto, ON: Bantum Books.

Gendlin, E.T. (1996). *Focusing-oriented psychotherapy: A manual of the experiential method*. New York, NY: Routledge.

Greenberg, L.S. (1984a). A task analysis of intrapersonal conflict resolution In L.N. Rice & L.S. Greenberg (Eds.), *Patterns of change: Intensive analysis of psychotherapy process* (pp. 67–123).

Greenberg, L.S. (1984b). Task analysis: The general approach In C.A. Rice & L.S. Greenberg (Eds.), *Patterns of change: Intensive analysis of psychotherapy process* (pp. 124–148). New York, NY: Guilford Press

Greenberg, L.S. (2007). A guide to conducting a task analysis of psychotherapeutic change *Psychotherapy Research, 17,* 15–30.

Greenberg, L.S. (2011). *Emotion focused therapy.* Washington, DC: American Psychological Association.

Greenberg, L.S., & Goldman, R.N. (2019). Theory of practice of emotion-focused therapy. In L.S. Greenberg & R.N. Goldman (Eds.), *Clinical Handbook of Emotion-Focused Therapy* (pp. 61–90). Washington, DC: American Psychological Association.

Greenberg, L.S., & Pascual-Leone, A. (2006). Emotion in psychotherapy: A practice-friendly research review. *Journal of Clinical Psychology, 62,* 611–630.

Greenberg, L.S., Rice, L.N., & Elliott, R.K. (1993). *Facilitating emotional change: The moment-by-moment process.* New York, NY: Guilford Press.

Greenberg, L.S., & Safran, J.D. (1987). *Emotion in psychotherapy: Affect, cognition and the process of change.* New York, NY: Guilford Press

Greenberg, L.S., & Safran, J.D. (1989). Emotion in psychology, *American Psychologist, 44,* 19–29.

Greenberg, L.S., & Watson, J.C. (2006). *Emotion-focused therapy for depression.* Washington, DC: American Psychological Association.

Harte, M., Strmelj, B., & Theiler, S. (2019a). Expanding the emotion focused therapy task of focusing to process emotional injury. *Person-Centered & Experiential Psychotherapies,* DOI:10.1080/14779757.2019.1618373.

Harte, M., Strmelj, B., & Theiler, S. (2019b). Processing emotional pain using the expanded Emotion Focused Therapy task of Focusing: A single-session case study. *Person-Centered & Experiential Psychotherapies,* DOI:10.1080/14779757.2019.1618372.

Hupbach, A., Gomez, R., Hardt, O., & Nadel, L. (2007). Reconsolidation of episodic memories: A subtle reminder triggers integration of new information. *Learning and Memory, 14,* 47–53.

Hupbach, A., Hardt, O., Gomez, R., & Nadel, L. (2008). The dynamics of memory: Context-dependent updating. *Learning and Memory, 15,* 574–579.

Izard, C.E. (1977). *Human emotions.* New York, NY: Plenum Press.

Lane, R.D., Ryan, L., Nadel, L., & Greenberg, L. (2015). Memory reconsolidation, emotional arousal, and the process of change in psychotherapy: New insights from brain science. *Behavioural and Brain Sciences, 38,* 1–64.

Levine, P.A. (2015). *Trauma and memory: Brain and body in a search for the living past: A practical guide for understanding and working with traumatic memory.* Berkeley, CA: North Atlantic Books.

McGaugh, J.M. (2000). Memory: A century of consolidation. *Science, 287,* 248–251.

Ogden, P. (2006). *Trauma and the body: A sensorimotor approach to psychotherapy.* New York, NY: Norton.

Ogden, P., & Fisher, J. (2015). *Sensorimotor psychotherapy: Interventions for trauma and attachment.* New York, NY: Norton.

Paivio, S.C., & Pascual-Leone, A. (2010). *Emotion-focused therapy for complex trauma: An integrative approach.* Washington, DC: American Psychological Association

Pascual-Leone, A., & Greenberg, L.S. (2007). Emotional processing in experiential therapy: Why 'the only way out is through'. *Journal of Consulting and Clinical Psychology, 75,* 875–887.

Porges, S.W. (2007). The polyvagal perspective. *Biological Psychology, 74,* 116–143.

Rice, L.N., & Greenberg, L.S. (1984). *Patterns of change: An intensive analysis of psychotherapeutic process.* New York, NY: Guilford Press.

Rice, L.N., & Saperia, E.P. (1984). Task analysis of the resolution of problematic reactions In C.A. Rice & L.S. Greenberg (Eds.), *Patterns of change: Intensive analysis of psychotherapy process* (pp. 29–66). New York, NY: Guilford Press.

Rossouw, P. (2013). The neuroscience of talking therapies. *Neuropsychotherapy in Australia, 24,* 3–13.

Rothschild, B. (2000). *The body remembers: The psychophysiology of trauma and trauma treatment.* New York, NY: Norton.

Rothschild, B. (2004, January/February). Applying the brakes: In trauma treament creating safety is essential. *Psychotherapy Networker.* Retrieved from https://www.psychotherapynetworker.org/blog/details/378/applying-the-brakes

Rothschild, B. (2011). *Trauma essentials: The go-to guide (go-to guides for mental health).* London, England: Norton.

Rubin, D.C., Berntsen, D., & Bohni, M.K. (2008). Memory-based model of post-traumatic stress disorder: Evaluating basic assumptions underlying the PTSD diagnosis. *Psychological Review, 115*, 985–1011.

Timulak, L. (2015). *Transforming emotional pain in psychotherapy: An emotion-focused approach*. East Sussex, England: Routledge.

van der Kolk, B.A. (1995). The body, memory, and the psychobiology of trauma. In A.J. Alpert (Ed.), *Sexual abuse recalled: Treating trauma in the ear of the recovered memory debate* (pp. 29–60). Northvale, NJ: Jason Aronson.

Chapter 7

American Psychiatric Association. (2013). *Diagnostic and statistical manual of mental disorders* (5th ed.). Washington, DC: Author.

Arntz, A. (2012). Imagery re-scripting as a therapeutic technique: Review of clinical trials, basic studies, and research agenda. *Journal of Experimental Psychopathology, 3*, 189–208.

Arntz, A. (2015). Imagery rescripting for posttraumatic stress disorder. In N.C. Thoma & D. McKay (Eds.), *Working with emotion in cognitive–behavioural therapy: Techniques for clinical practice* (pp. 203–215). New York, NY: Guilford Press.

Auszra, L., & Greenberg, L.K. (2007). Client emotional productivity. *European Psychotherapy, 7*, 137–152.

Auszra, L., Greenberg, L.S., & Herrmann, I. (2013). Client emotional productivity–optimal client in-session emotional processing experiential therapy. *Psychotherapy Research, 23*, 732–746.

Ekman, P. (1972). *Darwin and facial expression: A century of research in review*. New York, NY: Academic Press.

Elliott, R.K. (2010). Psychotherapy change process research: Realising the promise. *Psychotherapy Research, 20*, 123–135.

Elliott, R.K., Greenberg, L.S., & Leitaer, G. (2004). Research on experiential psychotherapies. In M.J. Lambert, A.E. Bergin, & S.L. Garfield (Eds.), *Handbook of psychotherapy and behavior change* (5th ed., pp. 493–539). New York, NY: Wiley.

Elliott, R.K., Slatick, E., & Urman, M. (2001). Qualitative change process research on psychotherapy: Alternative strategies. In J. Frommer & D.L. Rennie (Eds.), *Qualitative psychotherapy research: Methods and methodology* (pp. 69–111). Lengerich, Germany: Pabst Publishers.

Elliott, R.K., Watson, J.C., Goldman, R.N., & Greenberg, L.S. (2004). *Learning emotion-focused therapy: The process-experiential approach to change.* Washington, DC: American Psychological Association.

Elliott, R.K., & Zucconi, A. (2005). Organization and research framework for an international project on the effectiveness of psychotherapy and psychotherapy training (IPEPPT). Retrieved from www.communityzero.com/ipeppt

Elliott, R.K., & Zucconi, A. (2006). Doing research on the effectiveness of psychotherapy and psychotherapy training: A person-centered/experiential perspective. *Person-Centered and Experiential Psychotherapies, 5,* 81–100.

Ford, J.D. (2009). Neurobiological and developmental research: Clinical implications. In C.A. Courtois & J.D. Ford (Eds.), *Treating complex traumatic stress disorders: An evidence based guide* (pp. 31–58). New York, NY: Guilford Press.

Gendlin, E.T. (1981). *Focusing* (2nd ed.). Toronto, ON: Bantum Books.

Gendlin, E.T. (1996). *Focusing-oriented psychotherapy: A manual of experiential method.* New York, NY: Routledge.

Greenberg, L.S. (1984a). A task analysis of intrapersonal conflict resolution. In L.N. Rice & L.S. Greenberg (Eds.), *Patterns of change: Intensive analysis of psychotherapy process* (pp. 67–123). New York, NY: Guilford Press.

Greenberg, L.S. (1984b). Task analysis: The general approach. In C.A. Rice & L.S. Greenberg (Eds.), *Patterns of change: Intensive analysis of psychotherapy process* (pp. 124–148). New York, NY: Guilford Press.

Greenberg, L.S. (2007). A guide to conducting a task analysis of psychotherapeutic change. *Psychotherapy research, 17,* 15–30.

Greenberg, L.S. (2011). *Emotion-focused therapy.* Washington, DC: American Psychological Association.

Greenberg, L.S. (2015). Emotion focused therapy: A summary and overview. *EFT-Online, 1,* 1–26.

Greenberg, L.S., Rice, L.N., & Elliott, R.K. (1993). *Facilitating emotional change: The moment-by-moment process.* New York, NY: Guilford Press.

Greenberg, L.S., & Safran, J.D. (1987). *Emotion in psychotherapy: Affect, cognition and the process of change.* New York, NY: Guilford Press.

Greenberg, L.S., & Safran, J.D. (1989). Emotion in psychology. *American Psychologist, 44,* 19–29.

Greenberg, L.S., & Watson, J.C. (2006). *Emotion-focused therapy for depression.* Washington, DC: American Psychological Association.

Harte, M. (2012). *Change processes in therapy: Case studies in process-experiential/emotion-focused therapy.* La Trobe University, Melbourne. Retrieved from http://arrow.latrobe.edu.au:8080/vital/access/manager/Repository/latrobe:34721

Harte, M. (2017). *The use of task analysis to test a model of change for the expanded Emotion Focused Therapy (EFT) task of focusing.* Presented at the 2nd International Conference on Clinical and Counseling Psychology, October 16–17, 2017, in Osaka, Japan.

Horvath, A.O., & Greenberg, L.S. (1989). Development and validation of the working alliance inventory. *Journal of Counseling Psychology, 36,* 223–233.

Horvath, A.O., & Greenberg, L.S. (1994). *The working alliance: Theory, research and practice.* New York, NY: Wiley.

Hupbach, A., Gomez, R., Hardt, O., & Nadel, L. (2007). Reconsolidation of episodic memories: A subtle reminder triggers integration of new information. *Learning and Memory, 14,* 47–53.

Hupbach, A., Hardt, O., Gomez, R., & Nadel, L. (2008). The dynamics of memory: Context-dependent updating. *Learning and Memory, 15,* 574–579.

Izard, C.E. (1977). *Human emotions.* New York, NY: Plenum Press.

Klein, M.H., Mathieu-Coughlin, P., & Kiesler, D.J. (1986). The experiencing scales. In L.S. Greenberg & W. Pinsof (Eds.), *The psychotherapeutic process: A research handbook* (pp. 21–71). New York, NY: Guilford Press.

Lane, R.D., Ryan, L., Nadal, L., & Greenberg, L. (2015). Memory reconsolidation, emotional arousal, and the process of change in psychotherapy: New insights from brain science. *Behavioural and Brain Sciences, 38,* 1–64.

Levine, P.A. (2015). *Trauma and memory: Brain and body in a search for the living past. A practical guide for understanding and working with traumatic memory.* Berkeley, CA: North Atlantic Books.

Llewlyn, S.P. (1988). Psychological therapy as viewed by clients and therapists [Abstract]. *British Journal of Clinical Psychology, 27,* 223–237.

McLeod, J. (2003). *Doing counselling research* (2nd ed.). London, England: SAGE.

McLeod, J. (2010). Case study research in counselling and psychotherapyLondon, England: SAGE.

McLeod, J., & Elliott, R.K. (2011). Systematic case study research: A practice-orientated introduction to building an evidence base for counselling and psychotherapy. *Counselling and Psychotherapy Research, 11,* 1–10.

Missirlian, T.M., Toukmanian, S.G., Warwar, S., & Greenberg, L.S. (2005). Emotional arousal, client perceptual processing, and the working alliance in experiential psychotherapy for depression. *Journal of Consulting and Clinical Psychology, 73*, 861–871.

Norcross, J.C. (2010). The therapeutic relationship. In B.L. Duncan, S.D. Miller, B.E. Wampold, & M.A. Hubble (Eds.), *The heart and soul of change: Delivering what works in therapy* (2nd ed.). Washington, DC: American Psychological Association.

Ogden, P. (2006). *Trauma and the nody : A densorimotor spproach to psychotherapy.* New York, NY: Norton.

Ogden, P., & Fisher, J. (2015). *Sensorimotor psychotherapy: Interventions for trauma and attachment.* New York, NY: Norton.

Paivio, S.C., & Pascual-Leone, A. (2010). *Emotion-focused therapy for complex trauma: An integrative approach.* Washington, DC: American Psychological Association.

Porges, S.W. (2007). The polyvagal perspective. *Biological Psychology, 74*, 116–143.

Rice, L.N. (1984). Task analysis of the resolution of problematic reactions. In C.A. Rice & L.S. Greenberg (Eds.), *Patterns of change: Intensive analysis of psychotherapy process* (pp. 29–66). New York, NY: Guilford Press.

Rice, L.N., & Greenberg, L.S. (1984). *Patterns of change: An intensive analysis of psychotherapeutic process.* New York, NY: Guilford Press.

Rothschild, B. (2000). *The body remembers: The psychophysiology of trauma and trauma treatment.* New York, NY: Norton.

Rothschild, B. (2004, January/February). Applying the brakes: In trauma treament creating safety is essential. *Psychotherapy Networker.* Retrieved from https://www.psychotherapynetworker.org/blog/details/378/applying-the-brakes

Rothschild, B. (2011). Trauma essentials: *The go-to guide (go-to guides for mental health)* London, England: Norton.

Rubin, D.C., Berntsen, D., & Bohni, M.K. (2008). Memory-based model of post-traumatic stress disorder: Evaluating basic assumptions underlying the PTSD diagnosis. *Psychological Review, 115*, 985–1011.

Schneider, K. (1999). Multiple-case depth research: Bringing experience-near closer. *Journal of Clinical Psychology, 55*, 1531–1540.

Stiles, W.B. (2005). Case Studies. In J.C. Norcross, L.E. Beutler, & R.F. Levant (Eds.), *Evidence-based practices in mental health: Debate and dialogue on fundamental questions* (pp. 57–64). Washington, DC: American Psychological Association.

Timulak, L. (2015). *Transforming emotional pain in psychotherapy: An emotion-focused approach*. East Sussex, England: Routledge.

van der Kolk, B.A. (1995). The body, memory, and the psychobiology of trauma. In A.J. Alpert (Ed.), *Sexual abuse recalled: Treating trauma in the era of the recovered memory debate* (pp. 29–60). Northvale, NJ: Jason Aronson.

Warwar, S., & Greenberg, L.S. (1999). *Client Emotional Arousal Scale-III*. Toronto, ON: York University.

Yin, R.K. (2009). *Case study research: Design and methods*. Thousand Oaks: CA: SAGE.

Chapter 8

Elliott, R.K., & Greenberg, L.S. (1997). Muliple voices in process-experiential therapy: Dialogues between aspects of self. *Journal of Psychotherapy Integration 7*, 225–239.

Elliott, R.K., Watson, J.C., Goldman, R.N., & Greenberg, L.S. (2004). *Learning emotion-focused therapy: The process-experiential approach to change*. Washington, DC: American Psychological Association.

Greenberg, L.S. (1979). Resolving splits: The two-chair technique. *Psychotherapy Theory, Research & Practice, 16*, 316–324.

Greenberg, L.S. (1984a). A task analysis of intrapersonal conflict resolution In L.N. Rice & L.S. Greenberg (Eds.), *Patterns of change: Intensive analysis of psychotherapy process* (pp. 67–123).

Greenberg, L.S. (2004). Emotion-focused therapy. *Clinical Psychology and Psychotherapy, 11*, 3–16.

Greenberg, L.S. (2011). *Emotion focused therapy*. Washington, DC: American Psychological Association.

Greenberg, L.S., & Pascual-Leone, J. (1995). A dialectical constuctivist approach to experiential change. In R. Neimeyer & M. Mahoney (Eds.), *Constructivism in psychotherpay*. Washington, DC: American Psychological Association.

Greenberg, L.S., & Pascual-Leone, J. (2001). A dialectical constructivist view of the creation of personal meaning *Journal of Contructivist Psychology 14*, 165–186.

Greenberg, L. S., Rice, L. N., & Elliott, R. K. (1993). *Facilitating emotional change: The moment-by-moment process*. New York: Guilford Press.

Greenberg, L.S., & Watson, J.C. (2006). *Emotion-focused therapy for depression.* Washington, DC: American Psychological Association.

Moreno, J.L. (1946). *Psychodrama* (first Vol.). New York, NY: Beacon House. doi: http://dx.doi.org/10.1037/11506-000

Perls, F., Hefferline, R.F., & Goodman, P. (1951). *Gestalt therapy.* New York, NY: Dell.

Chapter 9

Csikszentmihalyi, M. (2002). *Flow: The psychology of happiness: The classic work on how to achieve happiness.* London, Engand: Ebury.

CPSIA information can be obtained
at www.ICGtesting.com
Printed in the USA
JSHW011553100523
41530JS00003B/111